TIME&TIDE

THE HISTORY OF THE SUTTONS GROUP

Philip R. Jordan

Matador
9 De Montfort Mews
Leicester LE1 7FW, UK
Tel: (+44) 116 255 9311 / 9312
Email: books@troubador.co.uk
Web: www.troubador.co.uk/matador

ISBN 978-1906221-508

Front: cover illustration: Alf Sutton with Horse & Cart: circa 1926
Back cover:: Modern Suttons vehicles

Typeset in 11pt Futura
Printed in the UK by Martins the Printers, Berwick-upon-Tweed, UK

Matador is an imprint of Troubador Publishing Ltd

I have been considering having a book written about the "Sutton Story" for several years now. However, in the spring last year, my MD presented to the board a breakdown of the group's history by decade. This cemented my thoughts for my father, the founder of the company, would have been a hundred in March 2007. I am also reaching a milestone with my sixtieth in the following year, so there is some justification for a little reflection. It has also been twenty years since my father passed away, and yet it is not only his memory that lives on, but a vibrant and dynamic company.

It is, however, not only the past that is fascinating, for there is a new generation active in the company and will perpetuate the story, and who knows, maybe in a few years time volume two maybe required.

The discovery of a Time Capsule, which my father laid down in 1961, will be opened, examined and then replaced. This time it will include a selection of artefacts from his five grand-children. During the research on the book an abundance of pictures, documents and other memorabilia has been recovered and has on more than one occasion bought a cheerful, and sometimes sorrowful, tear to my eye. If there is one thing about this story it is not without humour, and the occasional sorrow.

I have asked the author to be as candid as possible, but never wanting, or wishing, to cause any other persons upset, implied or otherwise. It is in essence a human story, and as with all such stories has joyous moments interspersed with traumas, some of which caused the family, and senior management, some grief. It is a record of the triumph of human endeavour and perseverance, coupled with a history of the company as well as a smattering of the history of the transport sector itself.

I trust the book will be read in the spirit it is written...for enjoyment.

Contents

Forward
Mr.A.M.Sutton   iii

Acknowledgements   vi
List of Illustrations   vii
Introduction   xi

1   The Early Years: 1907–1939   1

2   War, Politics & the Birth of Sutton & Son (St. Helens) Ltd: 1939–1954   11

3   Sutton & Son (St. Helens) Ltd: 1954–1978   19

4   Michael Sutton's Tenure and Alf Sutton's Death: 1978–1987   35

5   William Alfred Sutton: 1907–1987   45

6   1987–2007   59

7   The Future   65

     Appendix 1: The Wider Scene   67

     Appendix 2: The Cork List   77

     Appendix 3: Suttons Transport   79

Acknowledgements

The Author would like to thank the many people, employees, ex-employees, friends and family, who gave their time and copies of photographs and memorabilia.

Special thanks go to: Brian Weatherley, Editor-in Chief of *Commercial Motor* for his help and assistance in providing access to the CM archives.

Nynehead Books & Roundoak Publishing for their assistance.

List of Illustrations

Forward
Mr. Michael Sutton – Chairman, Suttons Group   iii

Introduction
Alf Sutton with Horse & Cart: circa 1926   xi
The Sutton family at Buckingham Palace – 1980   xiii
The Sutton Modern Fleet   xiii, xiv

Chapter 1
A typical scene at the coal face: circa 1900   3
Tax Disc for A.B.Sutton & Sons first vehicle   4
"Big Boy" – Leyland Hippo   6
"Oh Boy" – AEC Mammoth Major   7
Alf & Ada Sutton on their wedding day – July 1939   8

Chapter 2
Ration Book & Note   12
SS John S Darbyshire   13
Debtors & Creditors of A.B. Sutton & Sons: January 1948   15
Pilkington Letter 1953 to W.A. Sutton   16
Letter from Chas. Davy: 1953   17

Chapter 3
Early Suttons wagon at Islington   19
A 'Wagon & Drag' Chinese 6 wheel truck & trailer: FDJ 965   21
TVW Vehicle: HDJ 125   21

Portolite in action, with a trailer 22
Atkinson's 10,000th Chassis & Menu 24
The Parbold Trials 25
Development of the Elton Head Site 26
Messrs. Ted & Phil Ryan by Clock Tower 27
Opposite side of the Clock Tower 27
Tom Knowlden & Alf Sutton in India 28
The Newly Completed Bungalow 29
Alf Sutton & Jack Darbyshire 30
Michael Sutton at the Royal Lancashire Show & helping with a digger 30
Michael Sutton in racing mode 31
Michael Sutton in culinary mode 31
The Queen's Jubilee Parade & Suttons Union Flag 32
Michael Sutton outside Suttons Training Centre: circa 1975 32
Suttons Bell ranger & Thank you note from the Chancellor 32
First 40 foot trailer & Jaguar 'E' Type 33

Chapter 4
Commercial Motor Article – "What price British" 38
Suttons 25th Anniversary 40
Pictures from the 'Rocket 150' celebrations 41

Chapter 5
Scalextric Cartoon 45
Calendar for August 1964 46
'ADO' Menu 47
Alf & Ada Sutton on lawn 48
Rolls Royces 50
Rolls Royce and Hovercrafts, and Michael Sutton in photographic mode 51
Sandiway Cottage 52
Article on young entrepreneur 53
Diane Sutton with her parents 54
Alf Sutton with eldest grandchild, Clare 54
Alf Sutton with grandchildren over Christmas 55
Vern Schuppan 56

Alf Sutton's 80th Birthday celebrations at Pilkingtons 57
80th Birthday celebrations at Pilkingtons 58

Chapter 6
Development of the head Office at Widnes 61
The Lloyds Committee Room, now Suttons Boardroom 62

Appendix 1
Advert – Morris Commercial 67
Article – Over 450,000 Commercial Vehicles – 1928 68
Article – Problems – 15-ton Leyland 69
Advert – Henley Air Cushion Tyres 70
Article – Real Economy – Solex 71
Advert – ERF, 1939 72
Floor Plan of the Commercial Vehicles Show 1954 73
Article – Sutton stands by its old friends 74–75

Introduction

The Suttons Group has an extraordinary story to tell. One could be blamed for envisaging the story was solely a 'rags to riches' tale of the founder, William Alfred Sutton. Not so, for even he was not the real instigator of the Suttons Group. He joined his mother and two brothers in a coal bagging and delivery service in the mid-1920s. The original name of A.B.Sutton & Sons, which lasted until nationalisation in 1948, was his mother's inception, Alice Beatrice Sutton.

Alf Sutton was dragged, kicking and screaming, into nationalisation but it shows the character of the man that his group, within the British Road Services (BRS), and which he managed, was regarded by many as the most efficient. In 1954 he bought out of BRS and set up Sutton & Son (St. Helens) Ltd, and the rest, they say, is history.

This story is based on archive research, interviews with family, friends and employees (past and present). Fortunately a three hour tape from 1979 by Alf Sutton has been invaluable in obtaining an in-sight into his own thoughts and ideals. Aficionados of trucks may be disappointed, as this book does not go into the technical

Alf Sutton with Horse & Cart: circa 1926

The Sutton family at
Buckingham Palace
1980

aspects of the transport industry, but looks more at the human element of the Suttons Group. In addition, an attempt has been made to put the reader into the context of the time, as sometimes historical events can be, and often are, misinterpreted when viewed from today's perspective. Out of facts come myths; out of myths come legends, and this book will try to unravel the mystique, without destroying the charm of the Sutton's story.

The book will look at Alf Sutton as a son, husband, father and grandfather. Almost without exception, every interviewee described Alf Sutton as a man of extremes, but also a man of indubitable character and ethics. He was also blessed with a strong marriage. It may not be politically correct nowadays to say this, but behind Alf was a strong woman, and without her he would not have been half the man he was. We shall also see what legacy Alf Sutton left, not only in the company itself, but his family. However, no man is an island and the Suttons Group would not be where it is today without the efforts of a lot of people, least of all his own family.

In 1978 his son, Alfred Michael Sutton, took over as MD. As can be expected in such circumstances Michael's modern approach to business differed from his father's views. However, despite a change in the structure of the company on Alf Sutton's death in 1987, the company went from strength to strength up to the late 1990s. Then a series of unfortunate events led to the Annus Horribilis of 1999. Not only had Suttons started to lose money but a fire, and the near loss of the beautiful old Lloyds Committee Room at Widnes, epitomised the situation in which the Suttons Group and family found itself.

The family dusted itself down and got up to face the challenge. The result saw the reversal in fortunes and the Suttons Group moving forward again at a pace. The next generation are now becoming involved with the company and are determined to write their chapter in history. The group has a clear vision and business plan

Vehicles in the latest Suttons fleet

whilst appreciating and adapting to the fluid and competitive commercial world. However Suttons still has that essence of a family company and they have not forgotten their roots. One interesting figure given to me by one of the family was, "in around eighty years Suttons has gone from one horse power, delivering coal in a 5 mile radius, to over a 100,000 horse power (Suttons approximate number of trucks * average horse power 250*420bhp), and transporting nearly all types of products around the globe...," but first, let's go back to that one horse...

CHAPTER 1

The Early Years: 1907–1939

In 1907 John Wayne and Katherine Hepburn were born; the first meters were fitted to London taxis; Albert Einstein developed $E=mc^2$; Brooklands, the first ever purpose built racing circuit was completed; a million pounds would be worth £87 million at today's value and on 4th March 1907 William Alfred was born to Thomas and Alice Sutton in Lea Green, near St.Helens Lancashire, their fifth and final child. However, only four survived to adulthood, which was not untypical for this period.

Alf was most certainly the apple of his mother's eye. It is evident from his own testimony that he idolised his mother, and he admits she spoilt him. His first recollection, he recounts on the tape, recalls the story of how he killed a cat at the tender age of four. At first it seems a most barbaric thing to have done, but it must be put into context. In 1911 there were no supermarkets and most people from Alf's family background would have grown and produced a lot of their own food: the outskirts of St. Helens was still a very rural area. A tabby cat had been killing the Sutton's chickens and his mother seeing yet another dead chicken exclaimed, "I wish someone would kill that cat!" Alf took her seriously and he recalls vividly stalking the cat and jumping on it from an embankment, killing it instantly. He proudly went and showed his mother the cat only to be given a serious ticking off, and a cuff round the ear, as his mother would be horrified at what the neighbours would say.

Alf lived at 7 Lea Green Cottages and went to a small school at Sutton Manor, and later Rainhill. Even from his formative days he was careful with money, never shirked away from work and his ambitions were being honed. His mother used to give him 6d ($2^1/_2$ p) for the bus to school, which Alf saved and chose to walk to school instead. This was after he had worked at the local farm milking! On one occasion he recalls he went pea picking with his mother and they worked from 5.00 o'clock in the morning till 7.00 o'clock in the evening. They picked 43 hampers each weighing 45 lbs. On the tape Alf gives a small sigh and says, "People just don't know what work is about these days."

Alf was not an academic and he recalls one particular teacher, an officious man, who kept telling Alf he would come to nothing. When Alf left school at 15 and with his hard earned savings, he bought a motor bike and would ride past the school at finishing time just to let the teacher see he was making something of himself. The other myth, which I could not substantiate, but epitomises Alf, was that another teacher did see something in him, and tried to help as much as she could. Years later, when Alf had started to make his way in the world, he did not forget what this teacher had done for him. He would go round to her house and share a bottle of his favourite champagne, Dom Perignon, with her. "Well," she would say, "you never did come to anything?" and they would both roar with laughter. Alf never forgot those who had helped him.

In 1920 his mother set up A.B. Sutton & Sons with the two eldest boys Arthur and Herbert, but Arthur was the main stay. She bought coal in bulk from the Lea Green Colliery and then bagged and distributed it locally. The business struggled to make ends meet especially in the summer months. It wasn't for the lack of trying as Alice also had the licence to sell tobacco in the area showing, once again, the entrepreneurial streak that Alf inherited. However, young Alf Sutton wanted to make some real money and went to the colliery to become a miner. His mother was distraught as she had other ambitions for her youngest, namely to become a wheelwright and blacksmith.

It is rare that Alf's father, Thomas, is mentioned in his memoirs and even then it is never in a complimentary manner. As a small boy he would visit his Uncle Will, his father's younger brother, in a beautiful house near Malvern. It was in fact a tenanted farm, but Alf wasn't aware of this at the time. He admits to being ambitious and the drive that forced Alf on in life is implanted here, and although he does not openly criticise his father, it is plain he did not have a lot of time for him. Alf went to try and find his first job in a larger colliery further away from Lea Green. He waited for a Mr. Chadwick, the 'kingpin' of the colliery, always doffing his cap every morning as Mr. Chadwick passed. After a few days he was eventually called in and when Mr. Chadwick discovered he was Thomas Sutton's son he didn't get the job; he thought his father was lazy. Alf then went to the Lea Green Colliery and eventually got his signing on papers with the princely wage of £3 10s per week. His mother had to sign the papers, as Alf was under age, and she sobbed, not wanting to see her favourite son going down the pit.

Alf did not work for long in the pit for after just over a year, the foreman called him a bastard. Alf had a strong sense of pride and dignity and promptly hit the foreman, "bang on the nose" he recalled. He was the fifth legitimate child and was not having his mother's name tarnished in any way. The foreman was prepared to forget the incident but Alf said, "I'm a bit stupid that way and see things through to the bitter end." The manager took the side of the foreman and confirmed he was sacked. The legend goes that Alf, in the 1960s, bought the colliery and promptly went in and sacked the very same foreman. This is highly unlikely, for although Alf did buy the colliery, the pit had been closed by then. However one senses he would have most certainly enjoyed the experience if the opportunity had arisen.

This setback did however allow Alf to join the family firm, which by 1923 was almost bankrupt due to a bad

Typical scene at the
coal face
Circa 1900

debt of £56 causing serious cash flow problems. Alf bought his brothers out and managed to arrange a year's credit from the farmer and blacksmith. The first signs of his commercial prowess were now surfacing. Alf soon returned the budding coal bagging business into profit and Alf claimed to be "top of the pops" with his customers. He also started carrying pitching stone to Sutton Manor and then he transported sandstone to Liverpool for the Anglican Cathedral; his haulage days had now truly begun. It could be seen as slightly to denigrate Alf's achievements by saying he was in the right place at the right time. No-one can ever argue Alf's work ethics and commercial vision, but the North West had minerals and a booming industrial base that was crying out for the likes of Alf Sutton. It would be better to say, 'Cometh the Time: Cometh the Man'.

Alf started to expand the business and he recalls his desire to buy a commercial vehicle, but his mother was resisting such a move. Then one day he saw two brothers, from a neighbouring garage with a 6-wheeler Morris Commercial, loading up 4 tons of tin. They were wearing a collar and tie while Alf stood there, his face black and clothes dirty, and he realised, as he watched the two men, that this was the way to make money.

One Friday afternoon he had delivered coal to a Mrs. Creswell, and he admits he would charm the well-to-do ladies as competition was quite fierce. As he sat having afternoon tea and scones he told her about his ambitions, to which she replied, "Well if your mother won't buy you a motor, then I will!" Alf recalls that this frightened his mother and she went with Alf to McLean & Appleton's, a company he was later to buy, to view a Coach Built 13cwt Morris Commercial.

There is another version being told about his first vehicle that it was, in fact, a '1 ton Ford-Toner' which he bought from the local fruiterer, a Mr. Moses, who was in financial difficulty at the time. Alf didn't hear clearly what Mr. Moses had wanted for the vehicle and whether it was £35 or £95. He managed to scrape together the £95 and careful not to cause offence, or pay too much, he asked if he could have £5 off. Mr. Moses shouted at him that £35 was a very fair price and he wouldn't take a penny less. A sheepish but relieved Alf pulled out of his breeches the due £35!

Appendix 1 shows details on the types of vehicle of the day and the numerous problems and the cost of running them. It also states the size of the UK commercial fleet in 1928, which is surprisingly greater than the HGV fleet we have on the roads today.

Tax Disc of Sutton's first vehicle, a Leyland Hippo DJ 5152

1929 was an eventful year. Donald Bradman got his first test century against England: The first non-stop flight from England to India took place: The Vatican became a sovereign state and the Dow Jones reached its peak at 381.17 on 3rd September. However on 24th October, the infamous 'Black Thursday', started the biggest stock market crashes in history. It was also a pivotal year for Alf for he realised he had to move to larger vehicles and he met with a Mr. Soly Royal, who owned Ex-Army Transport Ltd. Alf recalled that looking back he was like a lamb to the slaughter. They were based in Queen's Street, Manchester; just off Deansgate. He took a tram into Manchester but it cost him 9d in a taxi to find the place; he clearly had not ventured into Manchester before. He had to find a deposit of £415 for a very robust 6 wheeler Leyland 'Hippo'. (This Leyland Hippo is the accepted first motor lorry vehicle Alf had acquired, but in his tapes it seems he had bought others before albeit much smaller vehicles).

Alf bought the Leyland Hippo registration DJ 5152 on HP. The cost of this vehicle being over £1,700 prompted Alf to describe his situation, 'I was welcomed with open arms and given some cock and bull story about potential earnings. Mr. Royal showed me the earnings for a Speedy Transport vehicle: he failed to mention that he owned the company and I was completely taken in.'

The legend goes that Alf had another problem, his mother. The Hire Purchase agreement was £61 17s 6d per month, "which was a lot of money in those days". Mrs. Sutton did not approve of paying 'on tick', and her philosophy was if you can't afford it you shouldn't buy it. She therefore made him sleep in the cab until it had been paid off. I believe this story actually came from the fact Alf did sleep in the cab when he was delivering to London, to save money. However Suttons for most of its life under Alf rarely, if at all, took on any debt. This did on more than a couple of occasions back-fire, but his philosophy was always the same as Hamlet, "Neither a borrower, or a lender be."

It wasn't all bad for, as stated 1929 was a big year for Alf, and he met Ada Mildred Thomas, his future wife. He saw her one day on the road side trying to fix her bicycle chain. Alf watched and after a few minutes Ada stood back and kicked the bike over and strutted off in contempt. Alf thought, 'that's the girl for me'. So it was with great pride a few months later he went to the shop, where Ada worked, to show her his new acquisition, which he had now christened "Big Boy".

His first job was to Fords at Dagenham and he thought it was the end of the earth. It might as well have been for the Leyland's top speed was 21 mph, flat out! He had taken a friend Fred Craig with him and they slept in the cab after taking supper of steak & kidney pie and piping hot tea, a meal Alf recalls in minute detail. He also recalls that he was shocked that fuel had gone up to $11^1/_2$ d. (Yes, eleven old pennies and a farthing, less than 5p in today's money!). He rarely came back empty, even then, and he went to Nottingham to get a return load of butter.

Royal's company was also a clearing house and would place the business with the likes of Alf Sutton. Alf soon realised he had been duped and by now had talked to other drivers who were in a similar position. It mustn't be forgotten that this was at the time of the worst recession ever. Alf decided that he would go and see Mr. Royal. He went to Manchester only to be fobbed off by his secretary, who added insult to injury by saying there was no 'traffic' at present. Alf was not the man to be brushed aside and he remained on the premises. Eventually he met Mr. Royal on a stairway and taking him by the arm, "went with him into his room; he was most surprised!" recounts Alf. Royal tried to talk his way out of the situation, but Alf admits he didn't understand what Soly Royal was talking about, he hadn't even heard of the "Stock Exchange" at this stage of his life, but he left Royal in no doubt as to his disquiet on his acquisition.

The meeting did the trick, albeit Alf was not allowed back to the Queen's Street premises, so he had to

Alf Sutton with
a Leyland Hippo –
"Big Boy"

telephone in for his work. However some of the jobs given to Alf were poor. One such job was moving six tons of metal 'dross', which lacerated his hands, then to load up lard for the return. Alf soon tired of this and five months later took the board "Ex Army Transport Ltd" off the vehicle and went freelance.

Alf had reasonable success and eventually went to see Jim Miller & Co. in Water Street, Liverpool. Miller's had all the cable traffic from BICC at Prescot and Alf got them out of a spot of trouble, and therefore ended up

"Oh Boy" – AEC
Mammoth Major
Circa 1935

working for them for awhile. In addition a friend and shooting companion (and sometime poacher, allegedly!) got him some work at Orr's Zinc White at Widnes. In 1933 he carried out his first take-over as Arthur Leach got into problems on his HP and Alf bought a wagon and trailer from him. In 1935 he purchased a Leyland Cub, but two years later he acquired his first new vehicle an AEC Mammoth Major eight-wheeler, nick-named "Oh-Boy". It is reputed the name came from the words that Alf uttered when he saw his new eight wheeler, and it followed on nicely from "Big-Boy". Alf claimed it was the first eight-wheel rigid 'oiler' in St. Helens, or for the

Alf & Ada's Sutton on their Wedding Day –
shooting ducks at a fair: July 1939

non-technical, a diesel.

The picture on page 7 shows Alf's attention to detail, with the prime destination as London, painted proudly on the side. The AEC changed Alf's fleet as it could reach 30 mph, leaving his Leylands behind, and if he freewheeled down a hill he could reach 60 mph. Alf recalls, "The rushing air underneath the floor boards meant it was nearly impossible to brake as the pedals were jammed. It was not for the faint-hearted!"

Some detail of his life during this period have been preserved by numerous $1\frac{1}{2}$d 'Post Office Letter Cards' that he sent to Ada from 1931 to 1936. They are written in pencil and go into great depths of how he was still waiting to be loaded or unloaded. Despite the frustration and tiredness that is evident, his humour shines through, for as he slept in the cab he heads his letters 'Hippo Villa'!

By 1939 Alf was still living at home with his mother and his sister Ethel, and although he was very fond of his mother, time marches on. His mother even bought Alf a brand new Riley Kestrel to entice him to remain at home, but Alf knew he couldn't keep Ada waiting any longer; she had already been patient for 10 years.

On 31st July 1939 with the war clouds gathering in Europe, Alf married Ada at St. Helens Registry Office. The honeymoon was an afternoon trip to Blackpool and then, on his wedding night, he jumped into his wagon and took a delivery down to London. One wonders how many young brides today would have allowed such an event.

Alf described, in his tape, how tough it was in those days. Transport people were regarded as 'brigands' by most people, and there were no facilities such as service stations, even taking a call of nature could be problematic. Yet, he said, there was a camaraderie and integrity between the drivers which, he believed, is not there today. Drivers would have to be able to repair their own vehicles, literally on the roadside. They would ensure as little damage and wear and tear was inflicted on the vehicle as possible. It was not a matter of getting the sack but, in most instances, the owners couldn't afford to have the vehicle repaired. At this time to 'blow a tyre' was viewed almost as a crime and no self respecting driver would ever admit to such an act! (Although Alf did admit, somewhat despondently, to 'blowing one' in a letter to Ada in 1934). A driver's wages would be 48/- per week, that's £2.40p in our decimal coinage, however for the time it was a reasonable wage.

One story that has been recalled was a job he took on collecting half sides of bacon from Liverpool Docks and delivering them to Manchester. He had also obtained a job for transporting ingots of metal to Manchester. He had managed to rent a small area close to Liverpool Docks. In one day he would go to the docks and load up 10 tons of bacon and then go round the corner, to his rented area, and unload the bacon. Immediately he would return to the docks, but this time to collect ingots of metal. A surprised foreman would question him that, "hadn't he just been in to load up?" to which Alf would reply it was his brother!

He would then return to the rented area and re-load his vehicle with the bacon and ingots. Then he would wait until nightfall before driving to Manchester so the police couldn't see how overloaded he was. In short he manhandled 60 tons and drove for 4 hours in one day. If he had done that today and VOSA had stopped him, apart from the overloading offence, he would have infringed Driver's Hours regulations, the Working Time Directive and a countless list of Health & Safety infringements which would have almost certainly have seen Alf sent to prison!

It is difficult to envisage what it must have been like starting and building up a business during the Great Depression, and the physical effort that was needed as forklift trucks had not been invented. Life did have its lighter moments. Alf recalls he had a vicious little terrier dog during his coal bagging days. Its name was Spot, due to him having a big black spot over one eye. "He was a little beggar," Alf chuckles. "He used to round up all the bitches and chase off any dogs who came near, but the funniest thing was he was too little and couldn't reach most of the bitches, and used to jump and yap around them!"

Alf was now 42 and married. As war started he had three vehicles but his ambition was to grow, and that's exactly what he did.

CHAPTER 2

War, Politics & the Birth of Sutton & Son (St. Helens) Ltd: 1939–1954

In 1939 the Spanish Civil War ended, but then World War 2 began. Reading through Commercial Motor (CM) over the first 6 months of the war is quite an eye opener. In CM on 8th September 1939 the magazine starts, "So war has come…" Talk about British reserve! It also compares transport, or nowadays we would call it logistics, in Britain and Germany, and carries on:

"Germany is comparatively weak in respect of commercial vehicles…" I wonder what the writer would make of today's producers of trucks. The article does however recognise the German road system is remarkable and would allow a smaller amount of trucks to operate more efficiently. The main theme of the press at this time was fuel efficiency and the encouragement of alternative fuels, such as compressed coal gas. In addition the government of the day was not even considering increasing the unladen-weight limits, but as war broke the "leopard had to change its spots…" There clearly is also a heated debate going on about what is a fair rate for hauliers when they are being used for emergency hire. The inference from the article is hauliers are being well and truly stuffed! In the Appendix 1 there are examples of an advert of the time helping with fuel consumption and an advert for ERF where customer service and delivery is a key issue.

Alf Sutton recalled that despite all the advice to the contrary he went ahead and expanded. He bought McKinnell & Co. Ltd of Irlam, which had nine trucks, in 1942. In the tape he re-counts how there was talk of no fuel or spare parts being available and, as others looked to down-sizing their businesses, he expanded. 'Everyone thought I was mad,' he said, 'but I wasn't and it was the best thing I ever did in my life.' It rings of the great Howard Hughes who during the great depression, in the late 1920s, bought up as much as he could. Men of foresight always go against the tide, and Alf Sutton's vision is evident here. On page 12 is an example of the ration coupon and a note from a "W.F.I" who was trying to ensure Alf's life blood did not dry up.

Alf tells one story about the war that clearly could have had dire consequences, but the British sense of humour

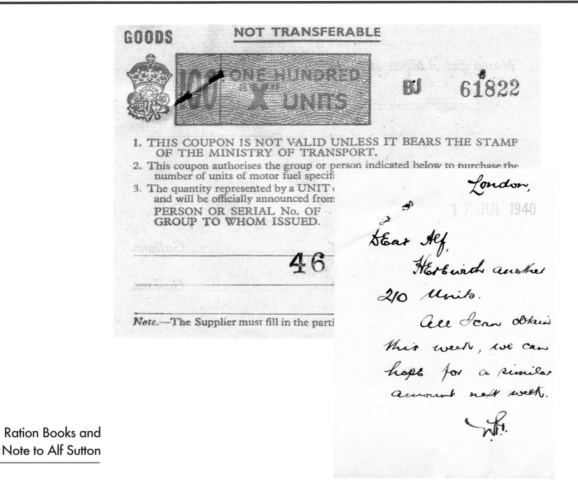

GOODS   NOT TRANSFERABLE

100 ONE HUNDRED "X" UNITS

BJ 61822

1. THIS COUPON IS NOT VALID UNLESS IT BEARS THE STAMP OF THE MINISTRY OF TRANSPORT.
2. This coupon authorises the group or person indicated below to purchase the number of units of motor fuel specifi
3. The quantity represented by a UNIT and will be officially announced from

PERSON OR SERIAL No. OF GROUP TO WHOM ISSUED.

46

Note.—The Supplier must fill in the parti

London,
17 JUL 1940

Dear Alf,
Herewith another 2/0 Units.
All I can obtain this week, we can hope for a similar amount next week.

Ration Books and Note to Alf Sutton

shines through. An old friend, Ginger Tomlinson, arrived at his house one day with five unexploded land mines on the back. A Marine sat with fixed bayonet on the back of the lorry and a WRNS officer with him in the cab. They were large cylinder objects the width of the lorry and had 36 brass nuts on the bottom and on the top were, 'what looked like the old 7lb weight.' Each one of the cylinders had been labelled as to where they had landed. Alf was fascinated by them and enquired if they were safe whereby the WRNS Officer retorted the 'teeth had been pulled.' As the ashen faced Tomkinson pulled away on his journey to Southampton another of his friends was scratching his head and asked Alf how come the Germans can be so accurate that they can put a label of the actual street on the bomb!

The upshot of all this was Tomkinson was delayed and by the time he arrived in Southampton an irate man in a white coat was screaming at him he had to go to a quarry within half an hour, or the bombs would explode. The truth has been nigh impossible to verify, but the story was re-counted by so many interviewees, that it does seem to have some credence.

Suttons Group was not built by one man alone and during this time Alf met Jack Darbyshire, who was Divisional Manager for the Ministry of Transport and was in charge of Liverpool Docks & Port. Liverpool it must be remembered was one of the most important ports with the majority of American aid funnelling through this deep water estuary. Alf assisted in the moving of the gliders, known as the black widows, which were used during D-Day and other encounters, from Liverpool docks down to Brize Norton. When Sutton & Son (St. Helens) was formed Jack joined Alf on the sales and marketing side. It was to be a special relationship, for Alf described him fondly as one of those men who never worked for me, but with me. This relationship was cemented when Sutton's only vessel was named after him: *John S Darbyshire*, which moved Bulk Latex from Southampton to Antwerp in the early 1970's

A.B.Sutton & Sons came out of the war with 12 vehicles and very quickly Alf realised the winds of political change would mean that nationalisation was inevitable. Determined not to work for the socialists he prepared himself by buying McLean & Appleton, a Nuffield dealership and garage, on Prescot Road, St. Helens; however not many believed him when he said he was going to sell cars for a living.

It is interesting at this point to compare 1945 to sixty years later, 2005. Once again the major issues are tariff rates and charges and in the RHA's Roadway magazine in February 1945 it proposed a standard rate on a national basis. Little did they know then how this idea would blossom in the spectre of nationalisation a few

The SS John S Darbyshire

years later. In 1945 there were just over 2 million vehicles on the road compared to 2005 where a 15 fold increase meant over 31 million now use our roads. Vehicles per mile of road however only increased five fold, but buses and coaches barely doubled. The greatest increase was cars which leapt from just under $1\frac{1}{2}$ million to 28 million, but trucks actually went down fractionally to 420,000.

Alf then made a move which countered his ambitions to move out of haulage with the pending nationalisation. Richard Pilkington also wanted to get out of haulage and Suttons took over 33 vehicles in 1947. The 1947 Transport Act was described by Commercial Motor on 15th August 1947 "...having been married in haste to a monstrous law, the public can look forward only to years of repentance.'

Alf resisted nationalisation and he claims he never actually took the voluntary purchase but, despite this, he did actually achieve the financial voluntary deal albeit on a compulsory basis. In 1948 A.B.Sutton & Sons and, its 44 vehicles, were bought by the nation.

Opposite are the Debtors and Creditors, as at 31/1/48, needed by BRS during the nationalisation process, but it is interesting to see Pilkington Brothers were by far the largest customer. On the debtors side fuel (The Petroleum Board!), tyres and parts were his main costs outside wages; not much different to today!

The deal Alf managed to procure was £387,000 and as he says in his own words was a 'substantial amount of money in those days'. Alf recalls taking a holiday with Ada and saying to her he could retire. Ada was aghast and said to him what would he do for the rest of his life, sit around? Alf knew she was right, for at this time Alf found himself a father. Alfred Michael Sutton was born on 19th August 1948, and just over 18 months later two days before his 43rd birthday Ada delivered a daughter, Diane Patricia.

Alf had bought a house not far from the depot, but the two could not agree on a name for it. After much heated debate it was named 'Loggerheads'! At this time Alf was not well for he had stomach ulcers and his surgeon advised he would have to cut out alcohol. The legend goes that the surgeon finally relented to Alf's protests but would only allow the purest of alcohol, and there is non purer, or so it was believed, than vintage champagne. Alf's main tipple from then on was Dom Perignon.

Alf Sutton's political colours had now been cast and they were most certainly not red, but he was a realist, and he decided to stick to what he knew. Major General Russell, the government inspectorate, appointed him manager of 6C St. Helens and Widnes (St. Helens) Group, in the North Western Division of British Road Services (BRS). However he did have a portrait of Sir Winston Churchill hanging behind his desk. Alf, once again aided by Ada, treated his region of BRS as his own, and soon his area became the envy of most managers, making over $£\frac{1}{4}$ million profit a year. It was during this time that a friendly rivalry built up between

Debtors and Creditors of
A B Sutton & Sons
January 1948

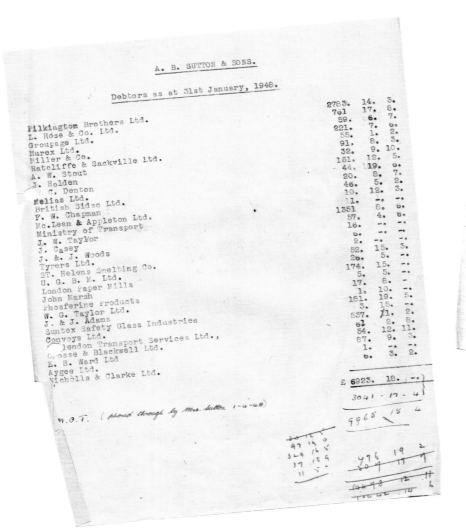

A. B. SUTTON & SONS.

Debtors as at 31st January, 1948.

	£	s.	d.
	2783.	14.	3.
	761	17.	8.
	59.	6.	7.
Pilkington Brothers Ltd.	221.	7.	2.
L. Rose & Co. Ltd.	55.	1.	2.
Groupage Ltd.	91.	8.	3.
Marex Ltd.	32.	9.	10.
Miller & Co.	151.	12.	5.
Ratcliffe & Sackville Ltd.	44.	119.	0.
A. W. Stout	20.	8.	7.
J. Holden	46.	5.	2.
C. Denton	10.	12.	3.
Melias Ltd.	11.	-.	-.
British Sidac Ltd.	1351	8.	6.
F. W. Chapman	57.	4.	-.
Mc.Lean & Appleton Ltd.	16.	-.	-.
Ministry of Transport	6.	-.	-.
J. W. Taylor	2.	-.	-.
J. Casey	52.	15.	3.
J. & J. Woods	26.	5.	-.
Tyrers Ltd.	174.	15.	-.
ST. Helens Smelting Co.	5.	5.	-.
U. G. B. M. Ltd.	17.	8.	-.
London Paper Mills	1.	10.	-.
John Marsh	181.	19.	5.
Phosferine Products	3.	15.	-.
W. G. Taylor Ltd.	537.	11.	2.
J. & J. Adams	61	2.	8.
Suntex Safety Glass Industries	54.	12.	11.
Convoys Ltd.	87.	9.	5.
london Transport Services Ltd.,	1.	-.	-.
Crosse & Blackwell Ltd.	6.	3.	2.
E. B. Ward Ltd			
Aygee Ltd.			
Nicholls & Clarke Ltd.			
	£ 6923.	18.	-.

n.o.t. (phoned through by Mrs. Sutton 1-4-48)

A. B. SUTTON & SONS.

CREDITORS AS AT 31st JANUARY, 1948.

	£	s.	d.
F.W. Chapman			
Motor Carriers			
A.J. Reed	209.	15.	-.
E. B. Ward	19.	1.	9.
J. Holden	9.	7.	11.
E. Hughes	6.	1.	8.
Bellendon	16.	4.	-.
R. Heaton	9.	13.	5.
A.W. Fillis	5.	7.	6.
A. E. Verling	34.	15.	11.
W. F. Sherran	12.	12.	2.
H. F. Rippon	19.	9.	9.
Holden	96.	15.	9.
J. H. Sutton	136.	14.	5.
Pilkington Bros.	3.	-.	-.
W. G. Taylor (Champion)	110.	17.	11.
British Industrial Gases	14.	1.	3.
Greenwood Tyre	3.	10.	-.
Leyton Tyre	1.	15.	8.
Tecalemit	9.	-.	-.
C. C. Wakefield	118.	4.	6.
F. Mc.Quillan	1.	4.	7.
Simms Motor Units	101.	10.	8.
London Paper Mills	34.	16.	-.
Postmaster General	21.	4.	5.
London Rd. Garage	1.	5.	-.
Norris Henty & Gardners	20.	8.	11.
Transport Repairers			
Todd Brothers			
Atkinson	15.	1.	10.
C. Swift & Sons	7.	10.	-.
Petroleum Board	1.	6.	4.
Timson Brothers	116.	1.	9.
F. W. Chapman			
Weber Storage Ltd.	462.	10.	-.
Lyon & Pye Ltd.	31.	15.	6.
St.Helens Corporation	1.	18.	3.
Jamaica Garage	1.	10.	1.
T. Hesketh	6.	12.	2.
E.R.F. Ltd.	4.	9.	6.
H.M. Hampson	52.	17.	6.
Critchleys	13.	17.	6.
	109.	3.	9.
	4.	11.	-.
	£ 1856.	4.	3.

him and Ken Brown, who ran Kentish Town Group in London, to see who could achieve the most profitable region. This light-hearted rivalry turned into friendship and Ken also joined the new company in 1954. He initially worked out of a telephone box in Islington but, despite these inauspicious beginnings, the relationship continued for over twenty five years.

Alf, not content in acting just as a manager at this time, spent the years evaluating vehicle types and engines. His preference was towards the Gardner engine and the Atkinson chassis, which both showed they stood the test of time, and for many years Suttons remained loyal to these two brands.

Pilkington Letter to
W.A Sutton
1953

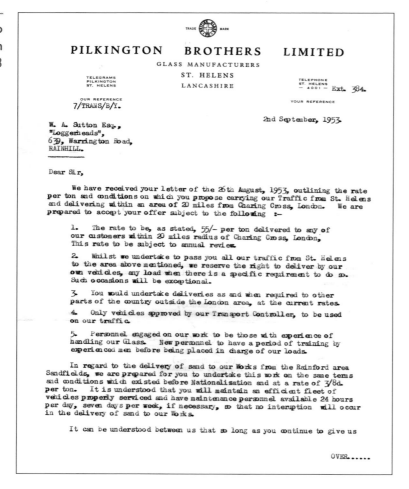

Politics once again had a part to play in Alf Sutton's affairs. In 1952 the Conservatives were back in power and the 1953 Transport Act heralded the return to free competition in long-distance haulage. Rumours abounded that BRS was to be completely de-nationalised. In addition technology and the road infra-structure was also moving on a pace and an Article in Commercial Motor on 11th April 1952 states, 'London to Leeds in three hours by road, cruising safely in a turbine-engined tractor-trailer with a 20-ton payload at 50-60 mph, sounds only a little less than inter-planetary travel, but in the foreseeable future it may be a mundane fact.'

Alf now saw his opportunity. On the left is a letter to Alf at his home address dated 2nd September 1953 from G.L.Bingham of Pilkington Bros accepting Alf Sutton's offer to deliver from St. Helens to London. To obtain the business Alf has had to offer the same rates as pre-nationalisation i.e. 5 years previously. He also had to provide maintenance personnel 24 hours, 7 days a week.

Opposite is a letter from Chas. Davy & Co Ltd,

where the search on the name Sutton & Son (St. Helens) Ltd had shown the name was free. This letter was addressed to James Jackson Esq. Alf had met James during the purchase of McKinnell & Co, as he was acting for them. Alf had been impressed and told Jackson he would like to take him on after the deal was complete. Jackson virtually ignored Alf as he thought he was trying to sweet talk him. Jackson would only talk to Alf after the deal had been completed, an act of integrity that impressed Alf. This relationship continues to the present day with James's son John still very much involved with Suttons.

Alf planned his strategy carefully and hand picked twenty of his best drivers, and now armed with the promise of a firm contract with Pilkingtons, he enticed them to join him. Rumours abound about the future of BRS and most of them knew joining Alf Sutton would be their safest option. Alf also tried to ensure the vehicles that he wanted were repaired and in tiptop condition, but just before he made his move they were removed to another depot and a rather dubious set of vehicles were now under his control. However, undeterred on Friday 2nd April 1954 Alf and his drivers, plus some administration staff, resigned en-masse from BRS. Then on Monday 5th April 1954 the drivers met at McLean & Appleton's premises and were then driven over to the BRS depot where Alf presented a cheque for 18 vehicles. Sutton & Son (St. Helens) Ltd had begun.

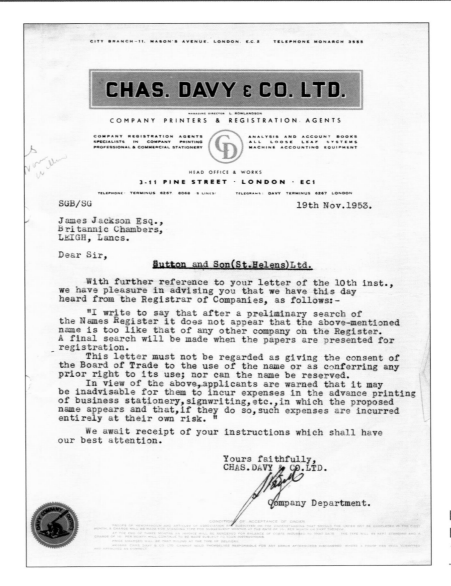

Letter from Chas. Davy & Co Ltd 1953

CHAPTER 3

Sutton & Son (St. Helens) Ltd: 1954–1978

1954 was another eventful year. The French army suffered a major defeat by the Vietnamese after the siege of Dien Bien Phu and Vietnam was divided. The first Commercial nuclear power station came on line in Obninsk, Russia and the Americans thought the Atomic bomb in Hiroshima wasn't destructive enough so they exploded the first hydrogen bomb, which was a 1,000 times bigger, on Bikini Atoll in the Marshall Islands. West Germany won the soccer world cup, Roger Bannister ran the first 4 minute mile and Oxford won the 100th Varsity boat race, and most importantly, Alf Sutton set up his new head-quarters at the Boar's Head garage, a property rented from Greenall Brewery, which is a stone's throw from the current Elton Head site, St Helens.

Alf had 18 vehicles and 58 people were on the first payroll. Already with him were some of his loyal employees Jack Darbyshire, Ken Brown, Bill Griffiths, Henry Pennington and Ted Ryan to name just a few. This was a time of change, development and innovation.

The changes can be clearly demonstrated in the Commercial Vehicle Show's ground plan for September 1954 (see Appendix 1). The list of exhibitors is a striking reminder of how the UK Truck manufacturers were effectively decimated in less than 50 years. By 1967 the first Scania trucks were being sold and the following year Volvos were available via agents Ailsa

An early Suttons Wagon at Islington

trucks, but despite this in 1968 the UK was still the largest exporter of trucks in the world. The self-destruct button, however, was about to be pressed and by 1971 the now newly formed British Leyland became a by-word for go-slows and strikes.

Change was also blowing through BRS, for although they did retain at least 76 depots in January 1955, the British Transport Commission had announced the sale of 149 depots and 5,830 vehicles. An article in Commercial Motor on 14th January 1955 shows the scale and, in some cases, confusion surrounding the sell off. It even states the largest fleet of 200 vehicles at Littlemore in Oxford had not been able to find a buyer, and that 'let the buyer beware', as many of the vehicles were in dubious condition. It was also evident that the RHA had been calling for the selll-off and the fact that BRS would be able to compete with free trade but backed by the tax-payer, was deemed unfair.

Development of the road system started in December 1958 with the first stretch of motorway being opened by the then Prime Minister Harold MacMillian. It is difficult to imagine that in 1965 there was no Severn Bridge and to reach South Wales from London would necessitate the use of the 'Aust Ferry', or a very long detour north.

However back to Alf Sutton, who had kitted out his vehicles with new ropes and sheets, and the famous Suttons night trunk to London began. The night trunk driver was respected within the organisation and by day the vehicles would be unloaded and re-loaded by 'day shunters'. Ken Brown was managing the London opera-tion, albeit from his office of a telephone booth, helping secure back deliveries. At this time glass, newsprint, paint and timber board were the staple loads for Suttons and this was to remain so for several years. Pilkington Glass and ICI were his two biggest customers. Sutton's however earned their growth and they had a reputation for never missing an overnight delivery, which was certainly appreciated by ICI, and allowed Suttons to expand their trade with them. Suttons were using the Atkinson eight wheeled rigid which was their flag ship and was still in use some thirty years later.

Alf looked at plans to expand north of the border. However this posed a problem for at this time, when the old A6 over Shap was a treacherous road, most drivers refused to negotiate it at the dead of night. As usual Alf persuaded one of his loyal drivers to take the task on and soon Glasgow was added to Sutton's network and the livery altered accordingly.

Also, at about this time, Alf's innovation and ingenuity were coming into play. Firstly he adapted his 6 wheeler fleet in such a way they could carry 4 tons more. He then added a trailer; a combination described as a 'wagon and drag' and obtained a legal payload of 22 tons, substantially more than the competition.

Secondly, Alf sought to build his own vehicles. He and a few other likeminded entrepreneurs namely, Eric

Green, Tom Ward and Stewart Eden-Smith developed TVW, Transport Vehicles (Warrington) Ltd. They only produced 6-7 vehicles and the picture below shows a vehicle with no maker's badge but was probably based on a Sentinel design and a Boalloy Cab.

Thirdly he invented and developed the 'Portolite', in short this was a large rubber bag with hole on the top and an outlet valve on the side. These bags were used primarily for hauling Tallow Oil. They could however be stored and the vehicle could be utilised to haul solids one way and fluids on the return or visa-versa. The system was so versatile that a triangle was often used using two Portolite bags.

In 1958 Suttons formed Anglo European Transport Services Ltd, which in turn formed British European Transport Ltd, which had very modest beginnings with a profit of only £4,655. 2s. 4d. in its first year. However the old adage states that from acorns mighty oaks grow,

A "Wagon & Drag" Chinese six wheel truck & trailer FDJ 965

One of the TVW vehicles HDJ 125

Portolite – Flat one
way-Bulk Back

which aptly describes this particular business, as it was the precursor to Suttons International, the largest division of Suttons current operations. The speed and diversity of the Suttons expansion is difficult to describe chronologically. He bought a coal mine (the very one he had been sacked from), a lead mine, brick works, farms and property. Alf was also at this time expanding his motor organisation and expanding not only McLean & Appleton but taking on new franchises. Sutton's Autos also had the Jaguar franchise in 1964. It was not the only mechanical horse power that Alf was interested in. He had a half share in a very successful race horse called Sovereign Park, which, during his ownership, won seven out of its five outings.

Strangely all this ingenuity had a price to pay from an unlikely source. Numerous articles in Commercial Motor starting on May 11th 1962 demonstrates the difficulties Suttons faced in applying for licences to use the Portolite. Despite being supported by Joseph Crosfield and Sons Ltd, he was opposed by the British Traffic Commission (BTC) and 'other private road operators'. It seems Alf could undercut them all by utilising his vehicles more efficiently. His applications continued a pace with ICI (Alkali Division & Dyestuffs division), Lever Brothers (Port Sunlight) Ltd and many others all supporting Suttons licence applications. Jack Darbyshire was vociferous in expounding the economics of Suttons developments, while the opposition, invariably B.T.C. and Pickfords, were now becoming desperate in their opposition. Suttons did get some licences but often at a much reduced numbers. Suttons once transported an Annigoni's portrait of the Queen, which Alf did for nothing. He claimed it helped in his bid for licensing when he had to declare all the types of goods Suttons carried!

A typical comment was quoted in Commercial Motor on 18th October 1963, by The North Western deputy licensing authority, Mr.A.H.Jolliffe who stated that although he did not want to hold back innovation he had to protect other hauliers from "undue competition". Alf's appeals were dismissed, and the Portolite patented idea had limited success; however it wasn't just the market that finally finished off the dual-purpose Portolite. The demountable tank-container had now started to supersede it, but in truth the rubber bag was difficult to wash out and was prone to puncturing. The experience with liquids did however help them to open new markets several years later.

Until 1968 it must be remembered that the A, B & C Licences were in force and any growth had to be justified to the Traffic Commissioner. In-addition Alf saw increased legislation starting with a campaign in April 1962 to undertake spot checks on lorry exhausts emitting excessive smoke. Also delays in loading and unloading led to another campaign by the RHA to "Turn that lorry round". However government legislation was starting to take a hold of the transport industry, which is still prevalent today, and a 32 tons gross weight limit was introduced in 1964.

Despite the knockbacks in the early and mid-sixties Suttons licence applications were gathering apace. These licenses were quite restrictive, with not only the customers being designated, but the radius the vehicle could travel and the product carried. Documents abound with details of vehicles and their licences, often being bought and sold just for a particular contract. As the market expanded the bureaucracy could not keep pace and finally, even the staunch Labourite Barbara Castle, brought in The 1968 Transport Act introducing the concept of 'Quality Licensing'.

Suttons had primarily been using Rigids until the early 1960's, but articulated lorries had started to enter the fleet and once again folklore recounts Alf's first encounter with an 'artic'. Suttons apparently bought their first 'artics' by accident when Alf purchased 17 vehicles of William Bros. of Peterborough. It was quite a mixed bag of vehicles and when they arrived at St. Helens, Alf eyed them suspiciously. One of his loyal drivers Bill Lewin, an advocate of the articulated lorry, had one loaded with glass bottles at the St. Helens depot. Bill tried to demonstrate to Alf how a load could be dropped with the trailer fully loaded, a real advantage with the delays in turning vehicles round at customer's premises. In his excitement to show off its prowess he had forgotten to wind down the trailer legs and pulling the release lever deposited the entire load of bottles across the yard. What Alf said is not documented, but it would have almost certainly been unprintable. However Alf Sutton saw the potential immediately and he embraced the new vehicle whole heartedly.

Signs of Suttons success came in unusual forms, especially in the press. One is an article in Commercial Motor on 22nd February 1963. It is headed: "Not selling!" The article claims that, the 150 vehicle firm from St. Helens, has attracted interest and take-over bids from several national road haulage firms. A spokesman, believed to be Jack Darbyshire, said, '...the interest...is probably because we are one of the few concerns of its type worth taking over, but the firm is definitely not for sale'. Confidence was high at Suttons.

The interest in acquiring Suttons possibly came from the simple fact that they were clearly a very profitable business. These profits were not a given right to Suttons; they were painstakingly earned. During the research through old documents a "costing" book was found. It breaks down vehicle costs by wages, fuel, tyres, maintenance, expenses and depreciation and the relevant percentages. It also shows the revenue and margins obtained. At the rear of the book is a six month survey from May to October in 1964, where different categories of vehicles are summarised such as General Chemical Tanks, Contract Trucks and the like. It is an interesting find as the most profitable business was ICI at Oldbury. What is astonishing is that during this six month period Suttons vehicles travelled just short of 4 million miles, and this was when the motorway network was very much in its infancy.

Suttons were held in high esteem by the industry at large and in the spring of 1964 Atkinson's chose Suttons for the celebration of their 10,000th chassis. A Sutton's vehicle was used in the promotion (left), and Alf was the guest of honour at the celebration lunch.

Alf constantly tested his vehicles to ensure he had the best and most economical vehicle on the road. Regular tests were conducted on the steep Parbold Hill near Wigan and two managers would sit on the back of the lorry whilst it laboured up the hill to ensure the tests were efficiently monitored. Below shows some pictures of the tests being conducted. This particular test was on a Gardner engine and shows Alf with Mr. J.K.Gardner. (Note the picture of the two men sitting on the load. The Health & Safety Executive would not be impressed.)

Alf wasn't just careful with his trucks, he was particularly careful about money, or more accurately, any unnecessary waste of it. He had

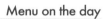

Suttons is used to celebrate Atkinson's 10,000th Chassis

Menu on the day

a reputation of almost meanness when it came to lighting, even to the point where he would go round offices and turn lights off whilst people were still working in them. Certain people adopted his philosophy to such an extent you would not be allowed a new biro until you brought the old one back, empty!

If Suttons prolific growth in vehicles was impressive then so was its expansion of depots and warehousing. The first major development was the Elton Head site: on page 26 is the site at Elton Head Sutton Heath and an aerial photograph taken at around 1967-8.

The 'famous' clock tower can be seen near the main gate with the two inscriptions:

Time & Tide waiteth for no man

The title of the book originated from Suttons being known as the company with the "Time & Tide inscription".

There is a tide in the affairs of man

At the main entrance is, what everyone knew as, 'the bungalow'. This was Alf's, Michael's and their Personal Assistant's offices. However a new Board Room was constructed at the rear of the main offices, and can been seen during construction in the photographs. Alf had also developed a site in Ireland Street, Widnes which served a purpose until the Elton Head site was ready. In 1961 Alf built a warehouse on the Elton Head site which was part of his plan to offer haulage

Alf Sutton chats to Mr Gardner

Pictures of the Parbold Trials in the early 60s; and Men sitting on the back

Development of the Elton Head site

and distribution. In the apex is a coping stone inscripted with "Erected by Sutton & Son (St.Helens) Ltd – 1961". In Alf's tape he mentions putting down a time capsule in the foundations of this warehouse and further investigation reveals that this capsule is actually behind this coping stone. At some stage this time capsule will be opened, examined but then returned, but this time it will also include a selection of objects donated by his grand-children.

In every story there are sad moments. In August 1965 a Suttons Caustic Soda tanker was involved in an accident killing three people. It was on a notorious black spot at Faversham, which had claimed the lives of a further four people in 24 hours. Fortunately the vehicle did not have any spillage and the accident clearly had an effect on Alf and his team with the emphasis on safety and high maintenance standards as a priority. This was followed by another of Suttons tankers turning over in Scotland, but fortunately this time no-one was hurt. Suttons successfully sued the Secretary of State for Scotland for badly maintained roads which had been the cause of the accident.

Suttons expanded their depots starting with Bethnal Green, Durham, Leicester,

Messrs Ted and Phil Ryan at the Clock Tower

The 'opposite' side of the tower

Oldbury and Manchester (Trafford Park) Billingham, Newcastle, Glasgow, Longtown. Such expansion can cause problems.

It must not be forgotten that in 1954 Alf started with around 18 vehicles, of which 16 were road worthy. By 1968 Suttons had a total of 222 vehicles, 99 rigids and 123 articulated plus 5 others. Alf's company car was listed as a Rolls Royce which in fact had been his standard vehicle for some years. This expansion and the fact that Suttons had always bought most capital equipment outright; they were suddenly confronted with a cash-flow crisis which even tested the resolve of Alf Sutton. Eventually, with some persuasion from the bank, he realised that the company had grown to a size that necessitated a CEO and a team of senior managers. The majority of this team did not last for long but the die was cast for Suttons to have non-family senior management. The seriousness of the crisis is demonstrated (see Appendix 1), with a letter from Pilkington Brothers agreeing to pay accounts on a twice monthly basis.

It was in 1965 that Alf Sutton joined forces with Tom Knowlden, a well respected freight forwarder based in London. Alf & Tom had become friends, as a picture below indicates, where they are covered in dye during a visit to India. Alf has from time to time shown a 'soft spot' for ex-military types and as Tom had been a Marine in France, seeing active service leaving him deaf in one ear; he fitted into Alf's plans. They set up an office at Bethnal Green and after initially engaged in general freight forwarding Tom moved them into demountable tank containers, starting with latex to Ireland and then moving the very hazardous Toluene Di-isocyanate (TDI) to Poland and expanding into Europe. He was the first to have tank containers cleaned out away from the home base and then obtaining a back load, often with food-stuffs inside.

Tom Knowlden and Alf Sutton in India

Alf had the money and drive while Tom's knowledge and contacts made the perfect combination for growth which continued for nearly 15 years. Tom however was still developing Boxley

Hotel & Restaurant, near Maidstone, Kent, trying to turn it into a country club. Tom therefore recruited a small band of managers that ran Suttons International whilst he played an overseeing role but still brought in new business. This informal situation would eventually end in tears, but for the moment Suttons International became a major player in International distribution.

In 1968 Alf Sutton's empire was not only growing inside the haulage company but he had been acquiring property. Another story is recounted in Alf needed to lay Lino at Rainhill. When Alf heard how much a square yard it would cost him, he quickly calculated it was dearer than land, and promptly went and bought farms, putting them out to tenancy. In 1962 he moved from 'Loggerheads' to Sandiway, just outside Hartford, Cheshire. Most of the depots were freehold as were various houses he had bought around the St.Helens site and rented them out, sometimes to key employees.

He had also bought Irving Little & Co. Ltd a painting and decorating outlet, based in Birkenhead, where Alf would only sell I.C.I.'s Dulux paint! A favour to one of his largest customers.

The "Bungalow"

Alf Sutton with his colleague and friend Jack Darbyshire

Michael Sutton at the Royal Lancashire Show; and helping dad with a digger

Turnover for Suttons in 1968 was just under £1.4 million and profits in excess of £300k, and a healthy balance sheet of £1½ million showing no liabilities other than a bank overdraft. The investment allowance shows his development of the Elton Head site. The following two pictures show 'The newly completed Bungalow' and the other is Alf Sutton with Jack Derbyshire in the Boardroom in 1968.

So what of the heir apparent? Well Michael, after prep school, had attended Malvern. At an early age he took an interest in the business, as the picture below demonstrates, and showing him standing in front of a 1954 Atkinson with a Gardner engine at the Royal Lancashire Show, in or around 1958.

Like his father, Michael took an early interest in cars and racing and the picture below shows a budding go-cart racer in the early 60's.

Michael had decided that academic life was not for him and, for a time, wanted to join the RAF. He had already obtained his Private Pilot's Licence (PPL), and passed his entrance exams to become a fighter pilot only to be frustrated by a failed medical due to his hay-fever. So, at the tender age of 19, Michael joined the business, and from the very start his interest and knowledge was impressive. In the summer of 1967 he went on a trip to Canada to learn about life and how business is conducted over there. A letter dated the 8th August 1967 discusses the pros & cons of different types of tanks and methods of loading and unloading. He also is telling his father about a new fibreglass tank which is three times stronger than steel, and are lighter and last longer. He also recommends a man that he met on his travels, for the technical manager's position at Sutton's. Clearly he was keen to make his mark.

However Michael had to earn his spurs and when he returned from Canada he had five years learning to be a fitter, welder, electrician and finally a clerk in the traffic office in Trafford Park and St. Helens. In 1973 Michael became a Director of Suttons and then in 1978 he was appointed MD at 30 years old.

This was just after he had instigated one of the best marketing initiatives in the transport industry. 1977 was the Queen's Jubilee year and Michael had his latest artic placed on her route with the front of the vehicle painted with a Union Jack. On a suitably positioned trailer, where Suttons staff were seated, a banner announced to the Queen: "God bless the Queen". It is said the Queen looked impressed by the new livery so Michael had the whole fleet converted and to this day, love it or hate it, Suttons is still known for this patriotic statement, although the Union Flag no longer appears on the Suttons vehicles.

Michael still however kept his interest in flying and Suttons Helicopters Ltd was formed and, with the

Michael Sutton in racing mode

Michael Sutton at his home showing some culinary skills

The Sutton vehicle at the Queen's Silver Jubilee Parade, which started the new Sutton's Livery

Michael Sutton outside Suttons Training Centre Circa 1975

Thank you note from Anthony Barber, 11 Downing Street

1st 40 foot trailer and E Type

purchase of a Bell Jet Ranger 206B, Suttons expanded into the giddy realm of air transportation. They also bought a three seater Enstrom. There were two pilots, one being Michael, and he had the honour of ferrying Tony Barber, the then Chancellor of the Exchequer, in June 1973 from Chequers to a function in the North of England, where he was MP for Altringham and Hale.

Michael wasn't the only son of a haulier learning the business. The young Edward Stobart was brought to St.Helens by his father to meet the 'famous' Alf Sutton. Alf it is said painted a gloomy picture of the UK distribution business, but the young Edward was not convinced and seeing Alf's professional operation gave the impetus to expand his father's business. It may have also been a rather sleek 'E' Type Jaguar sitting outside that bolstered the young man's ambitions!

In late 1978 Michael Sutton was MD of Suttons and the next decade was to see a formidable growth in new areas for Suttons, mushrooming legislation and a relationship between father and son that would change the face of Sutton's management forever.

CHAPTER 4

Michael Sutton's tenure
& Alf Sutton's death: 1978–1987

In 1978 we said hello to Louise Brown, the first 'test-tube' baby, the Sony Walkman and Bell's first cellular Mobile Phone. Interest rates were 11.75%, the film 'Grease' is premiered, and in London 'Evita' opens, while the Bees Gees are having a "Saturday Night Fever" at No.1. Sadly after 30 years we say goodbye to the Volkswagen Beetle after 20 million have been made, the oil tanker Amoco Cadiz founders off Brittany and Pope Paul VI dies, but arguably the most popular Pope, in recent history, John Paul II is elected the 264th Pontiff.

Michael Sutton at 30 years old, with three young children of his own, was now in charge of Suttons with a turnover of just over £11 million and healthy profits in excess of 10%. It is a period in Sutton's history which had many ups and downs, certainly on the human side and in the market place. All contributors to this book agreed that Alf & Michael, when working together, made an awesome team. Michael's natural charm and persuasiveness meant he was becoming more focused towards sales and marketing. However like his father before him he could also see the vision ahead and, clutching his instincts, he pushed hard for expansion on the International side.

Alf actually claims in his memoirs that he had intended to retire at 60 and now at 71 he should have handed the reins over to Michael. In 1980 he was awarded an OBE for Services to industry and it would possibly have been fitting for him then to take a back seat. It didn't happen, and an atmosphere built up between the two men that was uneasy, not only for Michael, but the whole management team. Michael viewed his father's continual interference as undermining him, while Alf was just not able to hand over full control. The relationship was, however, far from acrimonious. On one occasion Alf was so fearful for the safety of his son, whilst he was flying the helicopter that he insisted Michael ceased flying and the helicopter, was sold shortly afterwards. There is no blame being apportioned here as it is one of a long list of father and son companies that have had identical problems, and it is important the reader appreciates these tensions in understanding what happened in the next two decades.

A good example to demonstrate that the atmosphere was not too tense between the two men is the endearing tradition of 'the corks'. Alf Sutton liked his champagne his favourite label being Dom Perignon. During the research there was found, hiding in the corner of the old Board Room at St. Helens, a 'bunch' of champagne corks tied together, a label attached to each one. Appendix 2 is a list of the dates and the reasons for cracking open a bottle. Although Alf instigated this tradition it was Michael who kept it going, one of the very first being "Mike's well oiled birthday 19th August 1976".

However despite these tensions from 1978 to 1987 Suttons saw a dramatic increase with its turnover, nearly doubling to over £20 million, and importantly the margins remaining the same. The shareholders funds had matched the turnover by also doubling; so how was this achieved?

Firstly it is important to note the situation in Britain and the haulage industry at this time. It could be viewed that for the young MD, life had been handed to him on a plate. This was far from the truth for he may have had the trappings of the son of a wealthy man, but Alf demanded the same strict work ethics that he had lived by all his life. Michael's years of training within the company and the industry were assisted by a good management team around him. However, having Alf constantly around him as he embarked on the task of running the company was a situation that few would have been comfortable with, let alone endured. Michael's 'MD-ship' also experienced a baptism of fire as far as the changes within haulage industry started to unfold. Industrial strife, reams of new legislation, price wars, fuel shortage and 'contracting out' were events that had to be managed, not withstanding changes inside Suttons, that could have been catastrophic for the company.

In 1979 a diesel shortage was threatening the life blood of Britain. An article in Commercial Motor on 15th June 1979 reveals the fears at the time. The RHA & FTA were demanding action from the government, which was not forthcoming, and in addition the nationalised arm of the haulage industry, the National Freight Corporation (NFC), was seemingly doing a lot better with fuel than the private sector. How did Suttons cope? They bought many tanks and stored fuel to such an extent they eliminated worries about fuel supplies. They embraced diesel additives and considered all other fuel efficiency methods such as radial tyres and wind deflectors, albeit with a tanker fleet this was minimal.

One area of prolific growth at the time was legislation on employment. It could be thought today that this legislation has spiralled out of control, but the 'core' basis of employment legislation was laid down during this era. It was an area where Alf and Michael would have differing opinions as to how to run the business. The legend goes that Alf had a reputation for being a very tough employer, if anyone stepped out of line it would be "curtains for them". It is said that he once saw one of his vehicles with a tarpaulin flapping whilst he was driving home with Ada. He pulled the lorry over, sacked the driver on the spot, and telling Ada to follow, tied up the load and drove home. It also claimed that he once sacked a man in a service station for slacking. When the driver told him he didn't work for Suttons, Alf replied that wasn't an issue as he knew his boss. The driver it is said was duly sacked, such was the reputation of Alf. So the new approach that Michael took was one that took into consideration the realities of the day and on many occasion this riled Alf to a point where he interfered with Michael's decisions.

Legislation was not only confined to employment. In March 1979 the new safety and hazardous warning labels were introduced and, as Suttons was a major player in this sector, yet more administration and costs had to be incurred. In the same year the Tachograph was introduced. The more enlightened companies had already started to fit them as they saw the advantages of managing their drivers, but to this day it is still viewed as the 'spy in the cab'. This did have implications for Suttons, who were still running the nightly London trunk in that they could not get there and back in a night. So Suttons opened a depot at Padgate, Warrington and their efficiencies continued, only for the Driver's Hours to be increased and negating the necessity for Padgate!

Gross weight restrictions were also being examined with the UK's limit of 32 tons lifted to 38 on five axles, but it was to take to 1999 to reach the European limit of 44 mt. The industry hoped that the increased weights would impact on the bottom line, and for most it did, but in the wrong way.

In early 1980 the year dawned with a national haulage strike and the remaining nationalised part of the industry, NFC, was due to be privatised. The once mighty UK truck manufacturers were shrinking so rapidly they had practically gone before anybody realised it. Seddon Atkinson went into Spanish Ownership; General Motors closed Bedford while Ford sold their British arm to Iveco. The worst hit was the financially starved Leyland which shrank and names such as AEC and Guy were eventually dressed up in the merger of Leyland DAF. Margaret Thatcher was now squaring up to the unions and although industry bore the brunt, it was ultimately to be to the industry's own good.

If this wasn't enough, the RHA's theme for the 1980 conference was "Haulage in Crisis". Why? Well one of the main reasons was the particularly vicious rates war that was being conducted by the industry. A CM editorial on this rates war, 8th November 1980 said, "This is a civil war which claims-as all civil wars do-innocent victims where brother fights brother. Perfectly viable haulage businesses are going to the wall as long-established all well-serviced contracts terminate and not renewed". This was caused in part by contracting-out by the breweries and oil companies, and although a potential bonanza for the private sector, it turned into a blood bath. In addition the retail 'revolution' was starting to take place and a new and a more aggressive power base was developing as the supermarkets started to revolutionise storage and logistic thinking and operations.

Despite this Suttons remained loyal to a few suppliers. In an article in Commercial Motor on 15th December 1979 Michael and the then General Manager lay out why they were sticking with the Gardner engines and

VIEWPOINT

What price British?

BUYING British, however laudable a policy, is becoming ever more difficult for commercial vehicle operators. Part of the problem is a matter of semantics, or as Dr Joad might have said 40 years ago: "It depends what you mean by British".

Controversy surrounding the Britishness or otherwise of Volvos assembled at Irvine, as the result of protestations by Leyland in 1984, has never been resolved. The Society of Motor Manufacturers and Traders, as adjudicators in the matter, were faced with having to arbitrate between two of its members and suffered an attack of cold feet. Volvo chassis from the Scottish plant are now seemingly "stateless".

Perceptions of a vehicle's origins are inevitably flavoured by the manufacturer's parenthood. Hence Ford and Bedford trucks were, until last year, deemed by many transport users to have American antecedents and, as such, were regarded as less British than rival vehicles from say Leyland or ERF. This despite research and development as well as base manufacture being undertaken in this country.

Cataclysmic events have changed the face of the British truck industry to such an extent in the past 12 months that vehicle purchasing decision makers who are patriotically inclined now find themselves reeling in bewilderment. Bedford has gone and many of its customers as a first instinct have turned to Leyland rather than Ford or Dodge as an alternative.

Some undoubtedly saw Renault's ownership of Dodge and Iveco's new control of Ford as detracting from the British image of the product. But those (and there are many) who switched their orders from TLs to Freighters and from TMs to Roadtrains have been overtaken by DAF gaining a controlling interest in Leyland.

Had they known of Leyland's imminent Dutch connection, those erstwhile Bedford customers might well have given Italian-connected Ford and French-connected Dodge more sympathetic thought as options. They have now to face the fact that none of the contenders in the high-volume middleweight truck market is built by an all-British company.

It has been suggested recently that the presence of UK-based research and development facilities ought to be the determinant of a vehicle manufacturer's national status. So Ford, Bedford and Dodge, although foreign-owned for many years, all qualified as British.

Under the terms of both the Iveco Ford and DAF-Leyland "mergers", British-based R & D activity will continue. But, one asks, for how long? Advanced truck research work at Dunton is being wound down, leaving a much simpler development activity at Langley. The next generation of Dunstable-built middleweights will be called Renaults and developed in France.

DAF's plans meanwhile for the splendid Leyland engineering centre, completed only about six years ago at formidable expense, have yet to be revealed. If DAF and Leyland vehicle specifications are to be rationalised, as an obvious economy ploy, then a concentration of group R & D work in Eirdhoven is implied.

Only at 16 tons and more can the truck buyer now obtain a chassis from an all-British manufacturer, namely ERF, whose metaphorical Union Jack waving has understandably now become even more vigorous.

But wait. All the major powertrain components in ERF's successful new E-series chassis come from foreign-owned manufacturers. Cummins, Perkins (nee Rolls-Royce) and Gardner diesel engines are made in Britain – but by American or Canadian companies. Gearboxes from Eaton and Spicer, and drive-axles from Eaton and Rockwell, are similarly produced by UK subsidiaries of companies on the other side of the Atlantic.

Sadly then, the exercise of patriotism in the truck selection process is, in practice, now a barely-available luxury. The best that one can do is to look at the British labour content of available chassis before making a choice. On that basis ERF scores the highest marks, with some added assurance that profits, made in putting together those North American-flavoured major components, stay within our shores.

Alan Bunting

Suttons of St Helens flies the flag on ERFs

truck manufacturers Seddon Atkinson and the growing ERF. (See Appendix 1). The article is of particular interest as it lays out where Suttons were at this time. In short it summarised their car business, distribution, warehousing, International and the 300 demountable tankers and the budding rental business, which did in fact struggle. They had decided to stay British despite the market becoming flooded with foreign trucks. It was argued that despite the Gardner being more expensive it paid off in the long term, and that's what Suttons was all about. The Union Jack blazoned on the front of Sutton's vehicles may have looked a bit odd if laid over a Mercedes Benz star. However it did restrict Suttons to the two manufactures and on more than one occasion Suttons helped ERF sales in these difficult times ordering trucks before they were they really needed, taking advantage of capital allowances, and ordering in a fiscal year. Some things hadn't changed, for Sutton's 13 depots were still mainly supplied during the night and loaded during the day. Their system was effective and simple and allowed maintenance during the day on the vehicles. The article had significance during this time as a debate was being carried out by the industry, similar to the current discussions on Euro 4 & 5 engines, as to whether to go for the high torque, low rev engines as developed by Cummins, Rolls Royce and others.

A few years later, a Motor Transport article on 9th April 1987 debated the problem facing hauliers who want to buy British. Even The Society of Motor manufacturers and Traders couldn't decide if Volvo was British or not, due to their chassis actually being made in Scotland and as a result Volvo was deemed stateless! Even the only accepted British Manufacturer, namely ERF, had doubts about its origin as most of the components used were produced abroad. It was not a time to be patriotic in the haulage industry.

It wasn't all bad and Suttons still had time for fun. In 1979 Suttons celebrated their 25th anniversary and then in May 1980 Suttons became involved with the 150th anniversary of the Liverpool & Manchester Railway where the original trials were to compare Horse, steam and traction. Stevenson's Rocket Train underwent the original 'trials' at Rainhill in 1829. The celebrations however could have been curtailed as the wheels on the replica of the Rocket Train had buckled. So Michael Sutton and his Commercial Manager, Roger Boughton, came to the rescue and beating out metal wedges to straighten the wooden wheels and saved the day.

Another major event during this time was Suttons International business. In 1980 its turnover was around £3 million and was mostly being run by Tom Knowlden, Reg Lee, Stephen Jones and others. However the good relationship that had once existed between Alf Sutton and Knowlden was starting to falter. As already stated their commercial agreement had been over a handshake and nothing was recorded in a definitive contract: always a recipe for disaster. Tom had been developing a country house at the time called The Boxley Hotel and Country Club, and this combined with some personal problems had meant Tom wanted some money out of the business. It is not fair to debate this as both parties are now deceased, but letters at the time indicate a

Suttons' 25th Anniversary

Presentation in the Boardroom

Alf & Ada

Jack Darbyshire and Ada Sutton

The 150th Anniversary of the Liverpool & Manchester Railway – Rocket 150

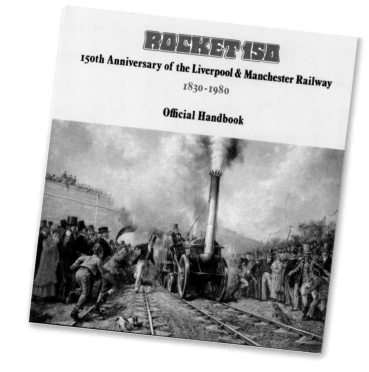

fundamental difference of opinion between the two men. Alf had financed the whole project while Tom had developed and run the business.

The problems with International were not to end there. In 1981 the four main personnel resigned en masse and went to their larger and main rival. It was a massive blow and this is when Michael, who had been standing back from the Knowlden affair, took control. Quickly recruiting people from the industry, the new team not only stabilised and rebuilt the business, but growth was possible again. Michael had been appalled by the utilisation of the de-mountable tanks on the spot business and went about ensuring that future tanks met a specification more suited to the market. Michael recalled how it was one of the occasions he had had a "barney with the old man." Alf thought Michael's meetings, discussing the specification of the tanks, were irrelevant and he should be out there running the business. This was met with a swift and silencing reply. 'Maybe, but at least we will be able to hire these tanks out.'

The tale of woe didn't end there for in 1983 Michael Sutton decided that International would be better placed in the North West at the Lea Green site. As usual in such circumstances, people rarely move with a job, and the team once again was dismantled and had to be rebuilt again, this time back at St. Helens. Other issues clouded the situation as the agent in the US was not performing, and although the business survived and eventually recovered, there is no doubt it suffered, especially if it is compared to the rapidly growing world market.

The market was also changing in terms of the financing of vehicles. The Conservative chancellor at the time, Nigel Lawson, was looking to remove altogether capital allowances against Corporation Tax. This would seriously harm an industry whose capital expenditure was so high, and although it was eventually modified it may have been the catalyst for the increase in the lease hire market, something that Suttons had to eventually embrace.

During the 'eighties' the growth continued, albeit with some rationalisation. They bought Smithy Haulage in Tan House Lane, Widnes in 1980 and opened depots at Billingham, and a new depot at Trafford Park, Manchester whilst closing the old Manchester depot and Durham. International now had offices in Tokyo. The Widnes site was opened and tankers are moved over there in 1985.

Suttons were however moving into new business areas obtaining new contracts with I.C.I. Paints division, BP and they even took control of the Guinness contract managing the rail-head in Runcorn and then Liverpool. So by 1987 Suttons were turning over £20 million, with profits in excess of £2 million.

Alf turned eighty on 4th March 1987. Despite his age and failing health he still came into the business most days, but by the summer he became seriously ill and died on 9th August 1987. However Alf did, and to some extent still does, speak from the grave. His Will left a legacy that, with perfect hind-sight, produced problems for the company and his two children. On the other had it has resulted in the third generation being 'cemented' together for the good of all. Alf had decreed that the business should be run by a board and empowered non-executives and trustees to act on behalf of the shareholders. A company, so used to the autocratic style of Alf Sutton, would now have to adapt to management by 'committee', a culture change which was going to prove difficult to control.

CHAPTER 5

William Alfred Sutton: 1907–1987

Alf Sutton, as already stated, was a man of extremes. He could be generous to a fault in one moment but the next he would be turning lights out, making people work in near darkness. He did not tolerate fools lightly, but also, on occasions, employed people of dubious ability. He engendered a loyalty from some employees resulting in fathers and sons working for him, and later on, Michael. There were those who viewed him as the archetypical capitalist, but even they still had a sneaking admiration for him.

Let's begin on a lighter note; his sense of humour. Alf Sutton had a Scalextric set in the loft of his home in Sandiway, supposedly for his young children, but I suspect this was a rue as during the research I found, in his papers, a post card which may have summed up the situation more accurately!

The Sutton & Son calendar of 1964 is a satirical look at all the roles within the company, and the month of August especially, shows the accountant, resplendent in a chef's hat in a kitchen 'cooking the books'. A pretty girl is adjusting a stocking with the caption that the accountant's first love is still 'figures'. (Interestingly the main marketing point is the Special Dual Purpose Tankers as mentioned earlier).

" I'm the M.D., damnit ! And I want the *red* car ! "

CHIEF ACCOUNTANT

Like most accountants, his manner is both mild and retiring. Note his obvious devotion to the task of cooking the books. He is a keen, dedicated man whose thoughts never stray from his first love, figures!

Sutton & Son
(St. Helens) Ltd
calendar
August 1964

Alf really liked a good 'do'. Opposite is a menu from, aptly called 'ADO' he organised in 1958.

Alf adored his wife, Ada. His letters to her have already been mentioned and although they were mainly practical in content, as he was often away for a week and more at a time, there is a tenderness that is unmistakable. Later, towards the end of their lives, he realised that Ada was not well with Alzheimer's and he tried to protect her from outsiders, and even attempted to keep it from the family. It was not until Alf had himself become ill and died that the rest of the family realised the seriousness of her condition. Alf had seen Ada's sister in a similar condition several years before and was determined Ada wouldn't end up the same way: but there were some things even Alf couldn't control.

What was Alf like as a Chief Executive? Clearly it is not possible to grow a business like Suttons without possessing a tough commercial acumen, but his hardness was always countered by fairness. Alf also passionately believed in providing the best customer service. There are many cases where Alf obtained business, even in the days of the A,B,C licensing, where he had identified the customer requirements, while BRS would have their customers fit in with their schedules. His first and major customer Pilkingtons had such respect for Alf and his service he became a bench mark of how a haulage and distribution business should be run.

'ADO' menu

SUTTONS & FRIENDS

HILL CLIFFE HYDRO: APPLETON

Chablis

Fio Pepe

Moët & Chandon 1949

Cockburns Port 1927

Chilled Melon
Fresh Lobster
Turtle Soup
Fillet of Sole Bonne Femme
Saddle of Mutton
Redcurrant Jelly
Sucking Pig
Duchess Potatoes
Croquette Potatoes
Cauliflower & Cream Sauce
Celery Hearts
Crêpe Suzette
Fresh Fruit Salad & Cream
Cheese: Celery Biscuits
Coffee

Biscuit Dubouche V.S.O.P

Liqueurs

ADO 30.1.58

Alf had the ability to manage from the visionary insight right through to the smallest, almost micro, detail. He would inspect the vehicles when they were parked up and would ensure they were in a perfect line. On another occasion Alf found a bolt in the middle of the yard. Storming into the fleet manager's office he demanded to know why he was throwing away Alf's money and wanted to know which vehicle it had come from! One particular example is a letter from the Rolls Royce agent in 1963. The 1961 Finance Act had imposed a taxation allowance on cars costing over £2,000, and a Rolls Royce at the time cost in excess of £5,000. Alf it seems was indignant that he should be penalised for buying an expensive British car. The letter, in a very delicate manner, answers saying an extra £290 tax paid by the company should not cause him any financial grief!

Alf and Ada Sutton on the lawn around the time of their marriage

As an employer Alf, once again, had his extremes. Suttons was not deemed a place for long employment and the number of people who came and went especially around the 1968 financial problems supports this view. However, on the other hand, Suttons have employees that have worked with the company most of their lives. Ted and Philip Ryan are two that must be noted. Ted is now 87 and spent many hours recounting his days working for Alf. On one occasion Alf needed something doing and Ted had to return from his family holiday in South Wales to fix it. It was almost expected of him but Alf was always fair and on other occasions Alf would hear through the grape-vine that Ted might need something, and quietly Alf would ensure Ted's needs were met. The loyalty and affection is such that his son Philip now works for Suttons in the same capacity as Maintenance Manager. Ted recalled that one day Alf saw, from his window, a vehicle supposedly parked up, begin to role out of control. Alf was horrified to see it was heading straight for Ted's office. He shouted to his PA to get Ted on the phone urgently. Eventually Ted answers the phone, but by then the vehicle had slammed into the side of the building, making Alf wince. "Are you all right?" he shouted down the phone. "Yes, Mr. Sutton, why?" Alf slightly flummoxed bellowed, "but didn't you feel that bang on your office?" "No Mr. Sutton I'm at the Oldbury Depot today..." The line went dead.

As has already been demonstrated Alf's work ethics were second to none. He went into work every day, virtually without exception. This occasionally caused a few problems when Michael's children came back from school during the holidays and, naturally, he would want to spend some time with them, especially at weekends. Alf just couldn't understand this as it was not in his psyche to let family interfere with work on Sundays. It was another example of the fundamental differences between them.

One of the author's personal recollections of Alf Sutton was a long discussion with him about friends. Alf stated that you will be lucky if you have as many as five true friends in your life, and even if you achieve this many you would have been blessed. The debate then centred on what makes a true friend and with a glint in his eye, "One that will bail you out when you are in trouble; at whatever cost."

Alf was recognised in 1980 for his work and achievements by being awarded an OBE for "Service to Industry." Alf was a Conservative supporter through and through and in a letter to Sir Alexander Douglas-Home at 10 Downing Street he implores the Prime Minister to inform the great British Public, in plain and simple terms, the successes the Conservative Party have achieved over the last 12 years. He ends the letter enclosing a cheque for 100 guineas!

Alf would have suffered in this present era of Political Correctness and delicate diplomacy. St.Helens was a hot bed of socialism and during one strike he had two of his Rolls Royces to drive across the picket lines during one of the strikes in the early 70's. He had had the number plates stuck on as WAS 1 & AMS 2, just to emphasise a point! These two Rolls Royces were pictured on a trip he took down to Monte Carlo for the Grand Prix (see p.50).

Rolls Royces

Rolls Royce &
Hovercraft

Michael the budding
photographer

Aerial view of
Sandiway Cottage

In addition he bitterly regretted that Sherdley Hall & Park in St.Helens, was bequeathed to the people of St.Helens after the death of its owner. Alf had always had his eye on the property and was horrified when the old house, he so adored, was demolished. They did, however, leave the old gates. He had to settle for Sandiway Cottage, which after renovation, was a substantial property nestled in the Cheshire Country side, but only a 20 minute drive from work.

There is a side of Alf that the world rarely saw and that was his benevolent side. On September 1963 in the newspaper, The Midweek Reporter, Alf gave a lesson to a 12 year old school boy who had dreams of making his fortune in the haulage business. An essay he had written mirrored Alf's life, and his English teacher felt he should inform Alf, especially when it transpired that the boy also saved his pocket money up. Alf, clearly, was impressed.

Alf was a dedicated supporter of Fairfield Hospital, which had originally been Guy Pilkington Memorial Hospital and helped in its construction and development. He also funded the renovation of the bell at Norton Priory as well as the bell tower at his local church.

One small but memorable part of Alf's life was his dogs. Apart from Spot, Alf had Alsatians (German Shepard) not only at the St.Helens depot, but at his home at Sandiway. At the depot the dogs would be let out once the gates were shut at the end of the day and only a few people could, or would, go near them, and these were normally the ones who fed them. Stories abound that on some occasions the tannoy would suddenly crackle into life and announce to be careful as the dogs had got out. There would be a scramble as people got into the safety of an office or cab. His grand-children all recall that Alf would take them walking with his dogs, especially a dog named Tim, at Sandiway and although he said they were harmless he still carried a sturdy stick and ordered them never to run. He had reason to for this dog gave Michael a nasty nip which needed stitches!

Alf by all accounts was a loving father but it seems accepted that he had a particular soft-spot for Diane. Whether this is because he viewed Michael, not only as son and heir, but also the future CEO of Suttons. Whilst with Diane he didn't have such expectations. This not a singular observation but one from nearly every member of the family. If Alf was a difficult and demanding father for a son, then it had its 'ups and down' being the daughter. Alf possibly saw some of the characteristics he admired in himself, or he had seen in Ada.

Article on young entrepreneur

Boardroom blues . . . John studies important business documents before meeting his directors.   (F3364/1)

JOHN JUST WANTS TO BE A MILLIONAIRE

Tycoon is impressed

SUCCESSFUL haulage boss, Alfred Sutton, gave a "future business tycoon" his first lesson on how to build up a big business last week. His pupil, 12-years-old John Naylor, who has dreams of making his fortune in the haulage business — just like Mr. Sutton.

And John already has a banking account. His assets . . . five shillings. That is how much he has saved so far for the purchase of an eight-wheel lorry of his own. He is just £3,999 15s. short of his target!

John's ambition was only discovered a couple of months ago, by chance. His English master at Central Modern School, North Road, set John and his classmates an essay to write on how they would "build up a business of their own."

In this way John, 13, Forshaw Avenue, Grange Park, revealed his ambition to become a haulage contractor.

He wrote that he would save as much pocket money as possible while attending school

Diane with her parents Alf and Ada

Alf Sutton with his eldest grandchild, Clare

Diane was astute, financially careful and had an air of confidence that must have melted his heart. But when it came to the choice of her husband, Alf did not approve. It is common for a lot of parents to feel their offspring's choice of partner is not exactly as they had hoped; but Alf stood his ground and even threatened not to give Diane away at her wedding. Diane was as tough as her father though and won the day. The relationship with his son-in-law was never easy and Stephen N. Broadhurst was possibly fortunate to be in the banking business and had no interest in joining a transport company. Unfortunately Diane and Stephen split up, but the marriage had been blessed with two children.

Michael's wife did not have such a tough time, if anything Alf had a great deal of time for Carol, and soon the third generation was being produced. Alf's favouritism for Diane continued for Tim Broadhurst, Diane's first born, remembers he spent a lot of time with his grandfather, but this may have been that Tim does bear a similarity in looks and build to Alf. However, Alf's favouritism never went too far; above is a picture with his first grandchild, Clare. The picture does tell its own story, for the look on Alf's face is of sheer happiness and contentment.

The grand-children's fondest memories of their grand-father were firstly Christmas Days at Sandiway Cottage.

Here are two pictures of the grand-children around the table and helping Alf to carve the turkey.

The second was how well he would scratch their backs and would seem to have an amazing amount of time for them, contentedly watching television with them. Even here the two grand-daughters recount the story that when Nicola was born, seven years after Clare, Alf told Clare that she was no longer his favourite granddaughter! His close relationship with his grand-children did have some positive aspects. They were all frightened stiff if they had a bad school report, as Alf would always examine them in much detail at the end of every term. Clare admits that without this 'threat' she would not have put so much effort in at school, and possibly would never have become a doctor.

Alf was also the Patron of the Isle of Man, TT Riders Association, which Michael subsequently took over from his father. Suttons also sponsored Vern Schuppan, who was a keen competitor at Le Mans, once being in a winning car.

Alf Sutton gets willing help from his grand-children in carving the Christmas Turkey... and enjoying it later

Vern Schuppan,
sponsored by Suttons
International Ltd

He also had an interest in St.Helens Rugby League Club. One evening whilst having a few drinks with some of the board members from the club it became apparent to Alf they were experiencing financial problems. Alf offered to buy the club outright and handed over a cheque! The next morning, when the effects of the alcohol had worn off, Alf's cheque was returned, but he was made a life member for his support.

On Sunday 9th August 1987, Alf passed away after a short illness. His obituaries in the local and commercial vehicle press all resound with his achievements from horse and cart to one of the largest private haulage, warehousing and bulk liquid transport companies. His determination and strong principles are highlighted and are evident in the company he left behind, and of course his recognition from the nation with his OBE. *The Truck* magazine in September 1987 couldn't help recalling his taste for cigars, which in fact he rarely smoked, and champagne, namely Dom Perignon. More interestingly nearly a quarter of the article goes into the two quotations on the side of the clock tower at St. Helens and their origins. 'The Time and Tide waiteth for no man' it states is a 16th Century proverb. It is in fact from the 14th century, but that is splitting hairs.

Alf Sutton on his 80th Birthday Celebration at Pilkington's Head Office 24th April 1987

It is the second and less known quotation that catches the moment in August 1987.

'There's a tide in the affairs of man,'

A quote from the Shakespeare himself, in his play *Julius Caesar,* and continues:

'Which, taken on the flood, leads to fortune;
Omitted, all the voyage of their life is bound in shallows and miseries.
On such a sea are we now afloat, and we must take the current when it serves,
Or lose our ventures.'

If this could ever describe one man; then it must be Alf Sutton.

Alf at his 80th Birthday Party at Suttons

1987 was not a good year. In March the ferry, Herald of Free Enterprise, capsized in Zeebrugge, October sees one of the worst storms in living memory hitting the South of England and the stock market collapses 26% on 'Black Monday'. For those now reaching for the whisky bottle they had more to endure with the King's Cross Fire. In addition we were to witness the Enniskillen bombing during a Remembrance Sunday Parade but more significantly our old bastion of defence, the English Channel, was being 'breached' with the beginning of construction of the Channel Tunnel in December. Alf Sutton's death also saw changes within the company that were to have significant consequences.

Mixed messages started to emerge from Suttons during this time. The investment made over the preceding 10 years had now started to produce results with turnover continuing to grow rapidly, profits remaining healthy with margins often reaching double figures, up to 1999, and then the problems began. Shareholder's Funds also tripled from 1987 to 1999 but, as with the profits, they also started to rapidly decline. The newly appointed Board or 'committee style' management, which was instigated in 1987, was alien to Suttons, and as the past ten years paved the way for profits for the future, so the new Board management structure led to the turn of fortunes by the late 1990's, compounded by a number of disastrous decisions.

Diane Broadhurst, Alf's daughter, had now also become more involved in the company. Diane had previously put her family commitments first, but now she joined the newly formed board. It is a difficult chapter for both Michael and Diane, and one that should and will remain private, save that, they were both experiencing marital problems, and there was a tension between the two siblings, caused by Alf's legacy, which fortunately for them, and the firm, was eventually resolved.

The old style of hands on management was gone and it has been said an air of malaise crept into the management, which later led to issues of poor financial performance and control and even a reprimand from the North West Traffic Commissioner. During research for this history many would tell the story how Alf Sutton would be seen whistling and shuffling along with his hands in his pockets. This was apparently a sign of agitation and sure enough he had seen something he had not liked and would delve into the matter with vigour. These 'intrusions' were, on many occasions, of little serious consequence; however it kept everyone on their toes. Many stories were recounted of how he would use his tannoy, calling to someone in the yard. A general manager from the 1980's said Alf had a knack of knowing if something was up, and would be on it like 'ton of bricks'. A man who instinctively knew how to manage by "walking the walk".

It was this slow change away from close micro-management that allowed certain elements within the business, such as costs, to suffer. Suttons had been used to the strict attention to detail and discipline, and slowly this detailed management of the business suffered. The next fifteen years or so was a frustrating time for the family and the board as they relied on their senior management and, in some cases, felt badly let down.

Suttons had now become less patriotic, not of choice, but simply because there were no real British truck manufacturers left, and the fleet increasingly moved over to Mercedes. It is an era where the unthinkable had finally happened, and Commercial Motor during this time had many articles and letters lamenting the passing of the once great UK truck manufacturers.

In 1990, as recession ravaged Britain, Nelson Mandela is released, Germany unified and the first Gulf war was about to start; the world looked a place of constant change. Yet during this time the haulage industry did remain amazingly buoyant despite, by now, becoming the most legislated industrial sector in the UK.

It wasn't all bad however. The weight limits were being increased and, despite the usual political in-fighting, roads were being constructed at a rapid rate in the late 1980's and early 1990's, albeit the density of traffic was still far greater than France and West Germany, and certain motorways were still very congested. The latest Leyland DAF 40 tonne vehicle now produced the same noise level as a BMW car. The smoke and emissions levels had and continued to be improved dramatically. In Commercial Motor on 4th March 1990 various people from the 'logistics' industry were interviewed about their predictions for the next decade. It is a gloomy read but it must be remembered that a recession was going on at the time. What was said then has uncannily similar echoes to today's problems. Legislation, pollution (emissions and noise), congestion, foreign truck manufacturers (as yet no mention of foreign truck competition on the roads) and of course profits, or more accurately the lack of them.

At Suttons there was also rationalisation with the closure of Padgate, London and Oldbury. The Motor Division was sold and Suttons went back to its core business. Suttons increase in turn-over was mainly down to International, however if this growth is compared, once again to the total market then Suttons were continuing to slip behind. Suttons owned or managed over 2,000 Tank Containers and offices were opened across the globe; the most significant one in Shanghai in 1997. This era also saw the head-quarters move away from St.Helens to the current site in Gorsey Lane, Widnes.

Development and construction of the new Head Office at Widnes: circa 1995

In 1996 Suttons secured the Rhone-Poulenc bulk chemicals business. It is around this time that Suttons bought the Ferns Tanker business. Ferns had been up for sale since 1995 and eventually had gone into administration and the acquisition turned out to be a terrible mistake, almost jeopardising the entire Suttons tanker business. Turnover may have almost doubled in three years but profits started to decline at an alarming rate.

Labour relations were also at a low and in the late 1990's Suttons were in dispute with the TGWU at their depots in Glasgow, Longtown, Staveley, Immingham, Avonmouth, Billingham and Widnes. The closure of Oldbury was also a factor and strike action seemed inevitable.

There is a rather apt old saying, "it never rains but it pours", and in 1999, Suttons were not over the worst. This year saw the loss of a major part of the Pilkington Glass business and the redundancy of 17 St. Helens drivers. On December 19th, a fire badly damaged the Widnes Boardroom, which had been painstakingly salvaged and restored from the historic Committee Room at Lloyds of London. A bleak start to the new millennium.

The Lloyds Committee Room at Widnes – Now Suttons new Boardroom

This was followed by further disturbing news that losses recorded in April 2000 were £3.7 million. The negative effect of the ill-fated Ferns acquisition; competitive pressures and continuing inadequate management performance had now combined and caused serious concern for the future of the group. Then in October 2000, the commercial problems of the road tanker business were further exacerbated by a second public enquiry in 12 months. This time the North West Traffic Commissioner curtailed the number of permitted vehicles significantly. Fortunately, as reported by the press at this time, it didn't materially affect the operation of the business.

The only bright spot was the recovery of the International business between 1999 and 2001 when a new Divisional Director, Andrew Palmer turned the business back into profit. He resigned and left the company in early 2001, but more on him later.

Losses escalated further to over £6 million for the year to April 2002 and concern had grown to deep anxiety among the family and Board. Changes and additions to the senior management had failed to improve performance. The business seemed on an inexorable decline with difficulties in key business principles such as cost control, debt collection, commercial contracts and operational management. All of these issues were then exacerbated by a strategic decision by Suttons to enter the UK gas and petroleum delivery markets. This decision was subsequently to prove costly, not only financially but also in management time. In 2002, even the International Division was experiencing problems. Then suddenly, on 29th September 2002, Diane Broadhurst died without warning. It was Suttons, and the family's darkest hour, but their determination and resilience, so epitomised by Alf, was to eventually shine through.

Despite the problems Suttons International had not been standing still. By 2001 the tank containers had grown to 2,250 and moving vast tonnages around the world. New contracts were being won by the group, such as Kemira Agro UK, and Suttons customers list was similar to the FT 100, in the industrial and chemical sectors. These customers were, in turn, also experiencing globalisation and were in need of logistics companies such as Suttons. Suttons were purchasing the new swap-body tank containers from Van-Hool, once again continuing Alf's philosophy of maximising the pay load.

However the Group performance continued to be unsatisfactory and fell short of shareholders expectations. So in late 2004 the board and specifically the Chairman, Michael Sutton, felt that a new impetus was required to move the group forward and consequently a change in senior management was necessary. In February 2005 Andrew Palmer rejoined the company, but this time as Group Managing Director. Andrew had kept in contact with the family since his departure in 2001. Suttons was now a large organisation of over £75 million but Andrew implemented changes rapidly and the effects of simple, but effective, management saw instant results.

By the July 2005 Motor Transport Awards Suttons had won the coveted Safety Award not once but twice. The improving financial performance now gave the board the confidence to support investment both in the tank container fleet and in replacement vehicles for the Tanker Division. In 2006 alone Suttons replaced over fifty vehicles, which was nearly 20% of the total fleet. Less obvious was an investment of over £1 million in their financial and operational systems, part of the plan to generate efficiencies. Alf Sutton would not have recognised the computer systems but he would have approved of the principles of their implementation. In April 2006 Suttons burst back into the black with a profit of over £2 million and a substantial amount of cash in the bank. Another performance indicator that would have impressed Alf Sutton. The press was full of articles about Suttons Chinese expansion, their growth in India and the Group's re-organisation. It was vital that the market, and most importantly Suttons' customers, started to view them with the confidence and respect they had once commanded.

Suttons also saw the third generation taking more senior roles within the company. John Sutton was appointed MD of International in June 2006 and his brother, Robert, is Director of IT. Tim Broadhurst, who spent ten years in the business learning his trade, has been assigned to the Shanghai office to develop the burgeoning domestic operations in China; emphasising how seriously Suttons view their future in this dynamic market.

In 2006 the new management team produced the first increase in Shareholders Funds since 1999, a trend that has been repeated in the year to 2007. Despite the fierce competition of the bulk chemical and gas markets, Palmer's style is simple and effective. His approach has been to impose discipline within the business, reduce costs, focus on cash collection, customer service and ensuring the commercial arrangements are equitable not only for the Group but its customers. Most importantly he has recruited a team of new managers who not only have seen increased performance across all aspects of the company, but lays a strong foundation for the future.

Some difficult decisions had to be taken not only with regard to former management but also the more 'mature' areas of the business, such as the St. Helens based Distribution Division, which increasingly is providing tenanted facilities as well as their traditional storage and haulage service. The Road Tanker Division has made dramatic improvements in controlling its costs and improving its utilisation and Suttons now have the reputation as the safest operator in this sector. The International Division has been perceived as the engine room of the future development of the group. Suttons are expanding their fleet and developing further into China, specifically in the Chinese domestic market and they have become the first Western logistics company to achieve the status of a wholly owned foreign enterprise in China rather than the more normal route of a joint venture. Palmer believes in Alf Sutton's principles of being a top service provider, with strict cost control, and more importantly to have the right people; then you obtain the right results. The management team have now secured the board's agreement to a comprehensive and detailed three year plan which sets out ambitious targets for all the divisions and a clear vision for the Group's future.

CHAPTER 7

The future

So what of the future? Suttons employ just short of 600 people and in Appendix 3 is a list of depots and offices throughout the world. Suttons own, or manage, 3,500 tank containers, nearly 450 road tankers, over 300 tractor units and finally nearly 450,000 sq.ft of warehousing.

The manufacturing engine room of the world is now China and the Pacific Rim countries, and words such as Globalisation were unheard of back in 1954. Technology such as containerisation and IT has opened up markets never dreamed of before. One thing is for certain that the situation will not remain static. It is difficult to predict what the future holds, but Suttons are committed to keep abreast of the market and ensure they are there with the right products and services to satisfy the needs of their customers.

This is not the place to quote the Business Plan in any detail but the Sutton's family are confident that there is a positive future and have committed themselves to further expansion. This, in all likelihood, will mean rationalisation in some areas, organic growth in others and substantial investment for the future. Like all sizable companies Suttons will continue to look at other opportunities to diversify, acquire or merge; it is dependent on market circumstances. Markets and industries have a habit of moving so quickly that any book would be out of date before the ink had dried.

In 2007 Suttons finds itself in the top 30 transport companies in the UK. It is one of the largest privately owned family companies and has not had to go to 'The City' to look for funds. At Suttons there still remains a family atmosphere, and a sense of history, blended into its business ethics. Suttons is proud of its past, diligent in its present and confident for the future. They are truly aware of the fact that:...

"Time & Tide waiteth for no man"

Chapter 1

Above is an advert for a typical vehicle of the day. Today the Road Tax is £1,200, mpg across the fleet is 8 but if you compare the payload, the modern vehicle is a lot more efficient. The most interesting fact about the advert is the 900-1,200 mpg for engine oil and it includes a speedometer!

It would be appropriate, at this point, to set the scene as to what life was like on the roads in 192?. Today there are just over 400,000 HGVs above 3.5 mt. In 1928 there were over 450,000 commercial vehicles on the road! Today we have 23 million cars but then only nearly 740,000. (See article below from Commercial Motor-March 1929). Some things never change and the article states that "the burden of increased taxation has been felt in the commercial vehicle world..."

Also about the same time another article examines a Thorneycroft 30-cwt lorry in the service of a Bolton oil concern. The article examines this vehicle due to its exceptional high mileage of 40,000 miles in 2½ years, and average of 16,000 p.a. Today's HGVs are averaging 150,000 miles p.a. In January 1928 Commercial Motor has another article about the 'Problems of the Haulier and

Morris Commercial Advert

Over 450,000
Commercial Motors in
Britain, 1928

Over 450,000 Commercial Motors in Britain.

WHILST there has been a substantial development of the motor movement in the year just concluded, the burden of increased taxation has been felt in the commercial-vehicle world, as is shown by the latest return of the number of licences granted during the twelve months from December 1st, 1926, to November 30th, 1927, those dates being taken because for all practical purposes the active licensing work of the year has then come to an end. Cars taxed on horse-power totalled 739,310, showing an increase for the year of 96,460. In the previous year the increase had been 77,110. Motorcycles increased by 20,612 to 518,867. For the first time in the annual returns electrically propelled vehicles are separated from other kinds. In 1926, 257,283 of all three types of goods vehicles (internal-combustion, steam and electric) were registered; in 1927 internal-combustion and steam vehicles numbered 279,857 and electrically propelled vehicles 1,415, so that the increase in the three types was 23,989. In the previous year that increase had been 25,326—not a serious difference, but deserving of attention.

The motor hackney vehicle (which term embraces the bus, the coach, the cab and the dual-purpose machine—sometimes goods and sometimes passengers—and the private-hire vehicle registered as a hackney carriage) has been reduced from 84,444 in 1925 to 82,677 in 1926, and now to 78,283 in 1927. Some of the "retirements" have been due to obsolescence and some to the fact that the public does not favour the van or lorry convertible to a passenger carrier by the week-end addition of a few chairs or forms, but without doubt higher taxation here tells its tale also.

Agrimotors have a microscopic increase of 98 to 16,402, and tractors used in agriculture and in general haulage have increased by 1,022, the number now being 3,878. Of the 18,920 exempted vehicles, many are fire-engines, ambulances, etc., and if we take 50,000 of the vehicles taxed on horse-power and 20,000 motorcycles as being employed in the course of trading, we get the substantial figure of 450,433 as the number of commercial motors in this country at the close of 1927, an increase of 50 per cent. seeming to have taken place in but the past few years.

Excluding invalid vehicles, tramcars and trade licences, the total number of motor vehicles represented by the licensing is 1,656,932. The number of driving licences issued during the year was approximately 2,349,000. In the last three months of the year (that is to say, to the end of November) the number of new vehicles registered for the first time was 50,672, of which 7,910 were goods vehicles and 1,507 hackney vehicles. Of the new goods vehicles the largest number was:—3,266 of under 1 ton capacity. Of new hackney vehicles the largest number was:—355 of a capacity not exceeding 40 passengers.

Carrier'. Below is a picture of a 15-ton Leyland-Carrimore, and the article concludes that bigger is better, more economical and makes more profit. It is highly probable that Alf Sutton saw this article or something similar for it states that some of the costs, mainly wages, are the same if you move one ton or fifteen.

The advert opposite, for Henley Air Cushion Tyres, emphasises how times have changed for the haulage industry. Basically it is a testimonial by Wiggs & Sons Ltd of Peckham. In December 1927 due to the Henley tyres a lorry was able to brave what seems like very bad wintry conditions on a round trip to Avonmouth. The advert boasts that they were able to do 255 miles in $2^1/_2$ days and this in itself astonished an A.A. official who was trying to persuade the driver to turn back. It would have been interesting to have a Tachograph in that vehicle as I am pretty sure the driver would have not only infringed the Driver's Hour Law but also would make the Working Time Directive look a bit sick.

Copy of the 15-ton Leyland from Problems article

January 24, 1928.   817   THE COMMERCIAL MOTOR

PROBLEMS OF THE HAULIER AND CARRIER.

More About that 100 Tons per 100 Miles, Showing How Economical it is to Use Big Units.

I DIGRESSED in my notes in last week's issue of *The Commercial Motor* from the problem under discussion the previous week, namely, that of discovering how best to carry a hundred tons a hundred miles every week. In solving this problem we are mainly concerned with the size of the units of the fleet employed. In fact, we found, after a brief preliminary discussion, that the problem resolves itself into a consideration of that point only, bearing in mind at the same time the importance of the factor of speed.

Twenty Tons at a Time.

For the first part of the investigation I chose as the unit a 12-ton, six-wheeled steam wagon, working in conjunction with an 8-ton trailer. This may be described as a 20-ton unit, and, to perform the allotted task involves five complete journeys per week. I found that three such units would be needed, two of them doing two journeys per week and the third only one journey. I worked out costs and arrived at an estimated cost of operation of the vehicles of £93 0s. 9d.

allowance was made in these calculations for establishment ... which, in a ... capable of ... a job of this ... could hardly be ... than £5 a week ... might very well ... A fair approxi-... figure, there-... for the all-in ... doing this ... with the three ... selected will ... a week or ... tons, and at ... figure, of course, ... could be no ... for the owner.

... for Profit.

... I should ... expect to gain ... £35 a week, ... probably ... get £20. At ... we may ... that he ... £20 and ... to get that. ... of profit ... cost and we get £120 as being the proper ... is equivalent to 24s. a ton.

... of interest, before we go farther, to work ... on a basis of a charge per mile. The ... covered by the three vehicles in trans-... 100 tons is 1,000 miles, since two of them ... of 200 miles each (including the return ... the third one journey. That means that ... works out at 2s. 4.8d. per mile. ... mileage is 10,000, being the product of 100 ... 100 miles. The cost per ton-mile is, there-

Eliminating the Trailer.

... we try to do without the trailer and ... any better results. The defect of the ... I have shown in previous calculations of ... that it decreases the speed of the whole ... ... thus affecting the possible weekly

mileage. The latter is a very important factor in consideration of cost, and it may be that by eliminating the trailer we shall be able to speed the vehicles up to such an extent as to make it more economical to do without them. The higher the useful weekly mileage the lower the cost per mile, other factors under consideration being equal.

Take, then, the six-wheeled steam wagon without trailer. The new vehicle has a capacity of 12 tons, so that for the conveyance of 100 tons per week 9 journeys will be necessary in that period. These will consist either of 8 journeys each involving a full load of 12 tons and a ninth journey carrying only 4 tons, or 9 journeys each with a load of 11 1-9th tons.

The first bull point in favour of the simple vehicle as opposed to the machine with trailer is scored when we come to discover how many machines will be required. The hundred-mile run will, with a single machine, be covered in a day. Each machine, therefore, will be capable of dealing with three loads per week, so that three machines only will be required for the work. The first cost will, therefore, be £3,900, so that an immediate saving of £600 is effected in this instance.

A 15-ton Leyland-Carrimore lorry recently supplied by Carrimore Six Wheelers, Ltd., for the transport of church bells and attendant gear for belfries.

Cost of Operation.

The cost of operation can be estimated as follows:— Tyres will be £160 a set and assuming that a set lasts 16,000 miles £2 worth of tyres will be worn away on each round trip of 200 miles. Fuel consumed at the rate of 10 miles per cwt. will involve a consumption of a ton of coal, plus, say, 1 cwt. for getting up steam— 21 cwt. in all, which is equivalent to an expenditure of 47s. 3d. if coal is 45s. a ton. Oil and grease will be, say, 4s. 9d., maintenance 19s., and depreciation 27s. 6d. The total running costs for one vehicle for one round journey are, therefore, £6 18s. 6d.

The weekly standing charges will not be very much less than those set out for the vehicle and trailer. The wages bill will be the same. There will still be 76s. for the driver and 65s. for his mate, giving a total of £7 1s. The maintenance allowance for these men will be a little less, since they will only be away from home three times a week instead of four. That figure will,

B43

A driver who did the impossible

WIGGS & SONS, LTD.,
70 HILL STREET, PECKHAM.
31st December, 1927.

Messrs. Henley's Tyre & Rubber Co. Ltd.,
20 Christopher Street,
London, E.C. 2.

Dear Sirs,

We had reason to despatch a lorry with a furniture lift (loaded) to Avonmouth on Wednesday last, the 28th inst., and feeling that it would interest you as the lorry we selected was shod with "Henley's Semi-Pneumatic Tyres," on account of the climatic conditions and also the slippery nature of the roads, we beg therefore to give you a few details of the difficulties experienced on the journey.

Our driver left Peckham at 1 o'clock midday on Wednesday the 28th inst., to proceed to Avonmouth, at which place he arrived on Thursday afternoon the 29th inst., where he discharged his load and left Avonmouth for London on Friday the 30th inst., and arrived at our garage at 8 o'clock the same day.

On the outward journey, in many parts, he encountered very heavy snow-drifts, and in some cases he had to make the journey across farms on the frozen snow, and come out the other side of the drifts which, in some cases, were nearly as high as the lift on his lorry, and he was told on his arrival at Bristol that he was the first man to come through since Christmas from London.

On his return journey, when he reached Fivefields, he was stopped by the A.A. official, who enquired his destination, and upon being informed London, he told him that it was an impossibility to get through, as nothing had been able to get through from London since Christmas. Upon our man informing him that he himself only left London on the 28th inst., and had reached Avonmouth and was now returning, he was nonplussed and could scarcely believe him, and told him that he had better proceed without further information.

In all, our man did 255 miles on the outward and return journey by way of a circuit run, which, in our opinion, is easily a record in two and a half days with such terrible climatic conditions prevailing, and we can only attribute this to the Spartan spirit on the part of our driver, and also that our lorry was fitted with "Henley's Semi-Pneumatic Tyres."

Yours faithfully,
p.p. WIGGS & SONS, LIMITED,
(Sgd.) JOHN WIGGS,
DIRECTOR.

HENLEY
AIR CUSHION TYRES

HENLEY'S TYRE & RUBBER CO., LTD.,
20/22 CHRISTOPHER STREET, FINSBURY SQUARE, LONDON, E.C. 2.
Branches : Glasgow, Bristol, Manchester, Newcastle-on-Tyne.   Works : Gravesend.
'Phones : *London Wall* 5394, 5395, 5396.   *Telegrams* : "*Hetewocol, Finsquare, London.*"

Chapter 2

Here is an advert from 1939 where a governor on the carburettor doubles fuel consumption.

It is a touch sad that a list of manufacturers in Commercial Motor on 1st September 1939 has some of the classic names. Austin Motor, British Tyre & Rubber, Dennis Bros., Fodens Ltd, Joseph Lucas, Jowett Cars, Leyland Motors... Some names are still with us today such as Ford and Shell Transport. Interestingly ERF, one of Sutton's favoured trucks are not listed but a few months later they take out a full page advert with a testimonial from a South African company (see page 72). Their sales pitch is customer service only, clearly an issue of the time.

Article on Real Economy, December 2 1939 – Solex

ERF advert of 1939

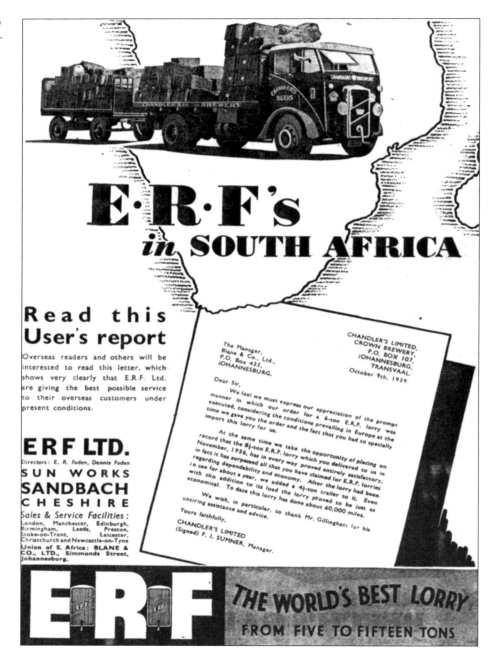

Chapter 3

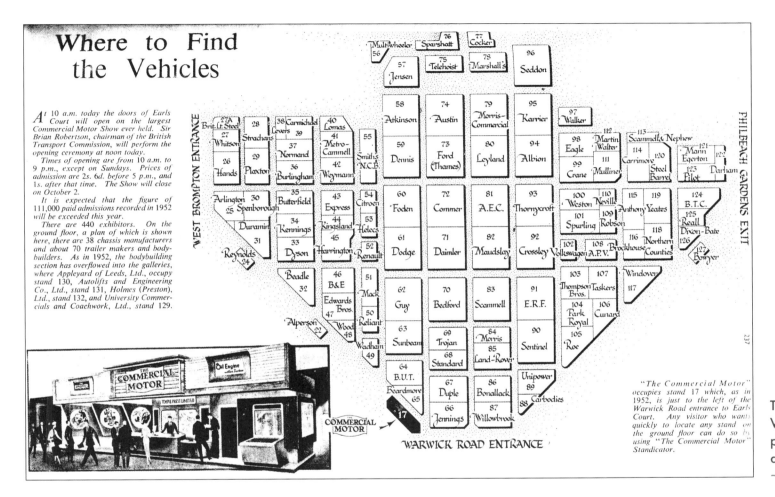

Where to Find the Vehicles

At 10 a.m. today the doors of Earls Court will open on the largest Commercial Motor Show ever held. Sir Brian Robertson, chairman of the British Transport Commission, will perform the opening ceremony at noon today.

Times of opening are from 10 a.m. to 9 p.m., except on Sundays. Prices of admission are 2s. 6d. before 5 p.m., and 1s. after that time. The Show will close on October 2.

It is expected that the figure of 111,000 paid admissions recorded in 1952 will be exceeded this year.

There are 440 exhibitors. On the ground floor, a plan of which is shown here, there are 38 chassis manufacturers and about 70 trailer makers and bodybuilders. As in 1952, the bodybuilding section has overflowed into the galleries, where Appleyard of Leeds, Ltd., occupy stand 130, Autolifts and Engineering Co., Ltd., stand 131, Holmes (Preston), Ltd., stand 132, and University Commercials and Coachwork, Ltd., stand 129.

"The Commercial Motor" occupies stand 17 which, as in 1952, is just to the left of the Warwick Road entrance to Earls Court. Any visitor who wants quickly to locate any stand on the ground floor can do so by using "The Commercial Motor" Standicator.

The 1954 Commercial Vehicle Show floor plan: Where did they all go?

Chapter 4

Sutton stands by its old friend

Despite being one of the foremost hauliers in the country, the lads from St Helens remain faithful to their first love — the Gardner engine. David Wilcox reports from the North West. Brian Weatherley took the pictures

FOREIGN commercial vehicles are taking a larger share of the British market than ever before — it is now 25 per cent — and Volvo, Mercedes-Benz and Scania are familiar sights on Britain's motorways. But around junction 7 of the M62 in the North West of England, the names ERF and Seddon Atkinson are likely to be more common. Junction 7 leads to St Helens, and the name of Sutton and Son is synonymous with that town in the haulage world.

Sutton and Son (St Helens) was, and still is, a family firm, now one of the leading haulage companies in the country. The firm has always been based in St Helens and its main depot and head office in Elton Head Road now covers some 13 acres which includes first-rate warehousing, offices, maintenance facilities and that valuable asset, hardstanding.

Managing director is Michael Sutton, while general manager is Richard Elviss. Richard first gave me a brief rundown of the company's activities, leaving until last the haulage business.

First, it is car distributor, a business that Suttons entered in the 1940s. These are mostly BL dealers in the North West but also include, in contrast, Ferrari distributors in Manchester, plus Mercedes-Benz and Ferrari in Huddersfield. A new venture in the car field is a Honda franchise in Southport.

Next, there is Suttons International. This is the Suttons company in the demountable tank business. It has approximately 300 of these ISO in-frame demountable tanks available for hire and used in the carriage of all types of liquid by road, rail and sea in the same manner as a conventional container.
continued overleaf

General manager Richard Elviss: "There is absolutely no merit in size alone."

Michael Sutton, managing director of Sutton and Son (St Helens) Ltd.

Below: One of Suttons' Seddon Atkinson units in the yard of the company's main St Helens depot. The distinctive Union Jack livery was adopted in 1977 to mark Jubilee year.

tainer. Suttons International merely supply the tank for hire.

In November 1978 Suttons Truck Rental commenced operation, and this heralded the arrival of several makes of vehicle that were new to Suttons. The Rental fleet has already grown to 115 in the first year and has over 30 Mercedes-Benz vehicles from panel vans to 32-ton sleeper cabs. The bulk of the rigids in the Rental fleet are Fords, but there are also some Leylands and Dodges. This break with tradition is due to the wider range of equipment that is demanded by the customer and the shorter vehicle life in truck rental, where vehicles are replaced every two years or so.

There are four rental depots, three at existing depots at St Helens, Manchester, and Bethnal Green, plus another rental-only depot at Ipswich. Birmingham is scheduled to open early in 1980.

At the heart of Sutton and Son is the haulage and warehousing operation. This is the rock on which the company was built, and it came across to me as a very solid base. The most immediately apparent feature of Suttons' haulage business is its vehicle policy. Suttons are totally committed to Gardner engines, not to one particular make of vehicle but to one engine manufacturer.

This arrangement dates back to the very beginnings of the company when both Suttons and Gardner were in their developing stages. Gardner engines were fitted then, and they have been ever since.

As a result of this Gardner policy, Suttons have been restricted to just two makes of vehicle which include a Gardner engine option — ERF and Seddon Atkinson. Both makes offer their top-weight tractive units for the British market with Gardner 8LXB 245bhp engine options.

And in all cases, for both the ERF B-Series units and the Seddon Atkinson 400-Series units, Suttons have chosen the Gardner option as opposed to the Cummins or Rolls-Royce engines.

What is the reason for this almost fanatical commitment to Gardner engines? "We think they are the best," said Richard Elviss quite simply. "Admittedly they are more expensive to buy in the first place, but we think it pays off in the long term. What we are looking for is reliability and long-life, and the Gardner fits the bill. This restricts us to ERF and Seddon Atkinson units,

but if the Gardner was available as an engine option in another unit I've no doubt we would [b]e at it.

In addition to being Gardn[er] fans, Sutton and Son ha[ve a] tradition of buying British p[ro-]ducts wherever possible, an[d] the ERF and Seddon Atkin[son] units are satisfactory from t[his] point of view as well.

Despite this pro-Gardner [pro-] British approach, Richard Elv[iss] said Suttons do not ign[ore] improvements or advan[ces] made in other engines [or] vehicles. The rental fleet, [for] instance, includes Merced[es-] Benz vehicles.

Their existence is explai[ned] thus: a truck-rental compa[ny] must take into account t[he] needs of its potential custome[rs] and many people could [be] attracted by Continen[tal] machines.

Suttons can also use the re[n-]tal fleet to evaluate the perf[or-]mance of different vehicles. [For] instance, there is a lone DAF a[nd] Berliet in the fleet at the m[o-]ment. So although the Sutto[ns] policy is quite definite, Rich[ard] Elviss emphasised that they [do] not consider it blinkered or u[n-]bending.

Suttons have around [100] units and 200 semi-traile[rs] working on general haulag[e.] Most of the trailers are 4[0ft] flats, predominantly by Cra[ne] Fruehauf.

Suttons lorries are eas[ily] spotted on the motorway — th[ey] are the only ones with the b[ot-]tom half of a Union Jack emb[la-]zoned over the front of the un[it.] This originated in the Quee[n's] jubilee year when vehicles we[re] painted in this livery to comm[e-]morate a Royal visit to [St] Helens.

But it proved so attracti[ve] that Suttons decided to retain [it] and it has since become t[he] colours for the haulage a[nd] road-tanker fleets. The fr[ont] fronts of the ERF and Seddo[n] Atkinson units accept th[is] scheme well, while the rest [of] the vehicle is in the usual Su[t-]tons red.

Rental fleet vehicles have [a] variation on this theme, min[us] the Union Jack, but with a wh[ite] stripe.

Suttons have 13 depo[ts] from Glasgow down to Sto[ke] market in East Anglia and Bet[h-]nal Green in East London. Sa[id] Richard Elviss: "There is abs[o-]lutely no merit in size alone [—] you must be able to offer a be[t-]ter service because of it." Suttons use their depot netwo[rk] to good advantage.

A glance at a map of the Su[t-]tons depots shows an empha[sis]

The truck rental fleet includes vehicles from panel vans to sleeper-cab tractive units, some of which are foreign. This is a non-hgv driving licence 7.5-tonne Mercedes-Benz 809.

This new road tanker was midway through being painted. Suttons have 190 tankers, many on contract work and some painted in the customer's colours instead of Suttons' red.

a few of the 300 demountable ISO tanks that Suttons International has for hire. e have electrical heating built in for the carriage of strictly temperature-controlled tances.

magnificent M-registered Atkinson Borderer has been completely overhauled and vated in the workshops of Sutton & Son, and was shortly to rejoin the haulage

the North West, the North st, the South East and the dlands. This spread is utilised the haulage trunking. hard Elviss unashamedly told that Suttons operates a atively specialised trunking edule, concentrating on the tes it can serve best: '99.9 cent of the journeys are rth West to London, North st to North East, North West Scotland and North West to st Anglia. For instance, we ely go down to the South st

Many of the journeys are also regular contracts and so the nking arrangements are rea-ably fixed, unlike a haulier o does a lot of one-off loads. Most of the trunk mileage is ne at night, with the loading d unloading carried out ing the day. Most of the runs olve night changeovers of vers. When an intermediate route depot is convenient for changeover, the trailer can

be dropped so that each driver can return to his base with his own unit.

If the changeover is carried out at a motorway service area, then drivers exchange complete outfits and they return to their depot eventually with a different unit.

Although a driver loses his regular allocated vehicle in these circumstances, it does enable vehicles to come into the bigger depots, particularly St Helens, for any more extensive maintenance that may be required.

Another advantage of the night changeover system is that drivers end up at their home depot and nights out are minimised. Carrying on from this, it also means that Suttons haulage fleet does not need to include sleeper-cab units, which has benefits in not only the cost of the vehicle, but also means that a bigger payload can be carried if needed.

Regular loads carried on the flat trailers in the haulage fleet include flat glass, glass bottles, paint, paper, foodstuffs and chemicals and powders in drums and sacks.

Richard Elviss told me why Suttons did not develop a 'go anywhere and everywhere' operation, which at first one might think a large company would do.

'We quite purposely concentrate on what we do best. Service quality is our strong point. We have a depot network that allows us to give good service on some main trunking routes, and this is what we do.'

In the past Suttons tried international haulage but feels that the market has since been saturated and the company has pulled out of international work.

To supplement the haulage services, Suttons also offer warehousing. At St Helens there is 400,000 square feet of warehouse floor space, some

racked up as far as five pallets high. Suttons warehousing services are varied.

They will carry out the complete warehousing function for a third-party customer if he requires, or at the other end of scale, will merely let the warehouse space to him and allow him control of his operation. United Glass and Nestlés are two of Suttons major warehousing customers.

Suttons are perhaps best known for their road-tanker work. The tanker fleet is based in the North West, at the Whitley depot between Warrington and Northwich. Here is the largest part of Suttons' 130-unit strong tanker fleet, naturally all Gardner-engined ERFs and Seddon Atkinsons.

Richard Elviss estimated that about 90 per cent of the road tankers are on regular contract work, mostly for the major chemical companies. All types of 'liquid chemicals, including

hazardous ones, are carried, plus such things as powders and edible oils. Suttons have close links with ICI and some of their depots are deliberately close to ICI plants. Indeed, Whitley itself is in an area where ICI is active.

The chief maintenance base for the company is at St Helens. Although the smaller depots also have their own workshops, major or more extensive work is done here. Richard Elviss said that the company is proud of its maintenance facilities, and after being shown roung the St Helens workshops it is easy to see why.

Suttons' attitude to maintenance is related to its vehicle policy. Because Gardners are essentially long-life engines, the maintenance is planned for long-term major overhauling. Similarly, the vehicles are bought outright and not leased, and so the company has long-term responsibility.

A guided tour of the St Helens workshops would begin at the pits where most of the maintenance is carried out. There is a separate overhead ramp arrangement outside for steamcleaning. There are also two lubrication bays in another building where this routine work can go on, leaving the pits free for repair and maintenance work.

There are also a number of specialised workshops at St Helens. In the engine shop and gearbox shop, power units and transmissions can be stripped down completely and overhauled or reconditioned. The engine shop is complete with overhead lifting tackle and track, plus a dynamometer for testing and running in engines after rebuilding.

Moving on, you come to the body shop. While most body shops replace the odd panel, this one is capable of virtually rebuilding cabs, and of course works on both the steel-cab Seddon Atkinson and the grp cab of the ERF.

During my visit, an M-registered Atkinson Borderer was almost ready to come out of the shop. The vehicle is seven years old, has covered around 750,000 miles, and was just starting its second life. It is a living testimony to Suttons' philosophy of buying quality long-life engines and carrying out major overhauls when necessary.

On general-haulage work, Suttons units cover around 2000-2500 miles a week and average about 7mpg — an economical consumption figure which justifies the company's

faith in the low-revving tenacious nature of the Gardner design.

In the paint shop was a new road tanker midway through being painted in the bright red livery. It was of the latest safety design, to a specification required by ICI. It had rubber suspension, roll-over protection and a centre-mounted tap; a location where it would not be knocked off in a rear end shunt.

The stores benefit greatly from having a one-engine and two-vehicle type fleet. Although the number of spare parts held at St Helens is impressive, it is reduced by the high degree of vehicle standardisation. The birth of the truck rental fleet with its mixture of vehicles, including foreign ones, has not caused as many problems in this department as one would at first expect.

Since the fleet is only a year old at the moment, the vehicles are still under warranty, so few parts are needed. Suttons also have a rolling road brake tester. This partially explains the company's interest in becoming an officially approved tachograph 'centre.

The whole maintenance organisation at St Helens is, without doubt, impressive. The only notable absence I could think of was a wrecker. But Suttons endorse their faith in their vehicles and workshops, and don't see the need for their own.

Richard Elviss said that on the rare occasions a vehicle did break down on the road, the company used commercial breakdown and recovery services. Another advantage of running on regular trunking runs is that they can develop the necessary contacts on the route over the months.

Richard Elviss readily admitted that Suttons' services do not come cheaply, but that service is the company's strong point. 'On our East Anglia to Scotland route we beat British Rail's freight service for speed on our overnight run.'

The rental fleet is like the 'provisional wing' of Suttons. It has grown from nothing to 115 vehicles in a year, and Suttons have shown themselves to be sufficiently flexible to give this division more flair and the more lively image that the truck rental market requires.

And there is one other rather unusual feature at Suttons that I should mention in passing. It operates a helicopter. A Bell Jetranger helicopter (available for hire) is based at the St Helens depot. No, it does not have a Gardner engine!

Printed by In Line Posting Ltd

The Cork List

Date	Celebration
1st April 1968	*Faded label*
5th April 1973	*Gordon Lightfoot's 35th Birthday & on 6th Suttons 19th*
12th April 1973	*Di Sutton's wedding*
12th May 1973	*Happy Birthday – Di Sutton*
4th April 1975	*21st of Suttons Many labels signed*
30th April 1975	*Defeat of Chancellor's CTT*
19th August 1976	*Mike's well oiled birthday*
10th December 1976	*To Nicola*
21st February 1977	*Janice Tinsley left, temporarily, to have a baby*
3rd June 1977	*I.C.I. Petroleum Group's 1st full meeting at St. Helens*
7th July 1977	*Jubilee Day*
7th July 1977	*Just signatures*
27th July 1977	*Lunch for Septuagerariam (or nearly)*
26th October 1977	*The Carlton Tower – Chelsea Room – Scotch Water*
1st September 1977	*Harry Lowe's Retirement*
12th November 1977	*Carol Brewer's 21st Birthday*
6th April 1978	*24th Anniversary of return into Transport*
11th April 1978	*The day we went into truck rental*
19th August 1978	*Mike's Appointment as MD*
17th December 1978	*"First bottle of the day"*

Date	Celebration
7th April 1979	*Inauguration – Renault franchise @ ROATAC*
April 1979	*25th Anniversary*
19th June 1980	*Visit of His Grace Duke of Westminster*
28th November 1980	*Ellen Blake's Retirement*
18th December 1980	*Ada's 70th*
4th March 1982	*75th Birthday Alf – Calendar "These are people..."*
14th March 1983	*Visit H.Kaeboosen & Heiszurga - Zeebrugge*
14th April 1983	*Visit Mr-Mrs-Miss Damien Fraser*
21st October 1983	*Arthur Guinness & Co – Distribution from Runcorn*
7th November 1983	Blank
10th May 1984	*Peter R. Chamberlain*
11th July 1985	*Visit of Lou Di Pasqua*
9th October 1985	*1st Lunch @ Nat West*
18th December 1985	*Ada'a 75th*
22nd March 1986	*Celebrate John D. Seddon to fold*
28th May 1986	*Semi-retirement of Bill Banks*
9th August 1988	*Happy memories of Mr. Sutton*
19th August 1988	*Mike's 40th*
5th October 1988	*Occasion of signing Hay's Glasgow Contract*
9th January 1989	*John Hendrey's 60th*
8th September 1989	*Commemorate sale of Sutton Motor Gp:*
26th February 1990	*To Celebrate the 65th Birthday – Arthur Jones*
26th February 1990	*Arthur Jones 65th (1 day late)*
9th March 1990	*Visit Bill Collins - OZ*
21st May 1990	*Ted Ryan 70th Birthday (1 day late)*
7th April 1994	*Ken Douglas Retirement*
12th August 1996	*Award Rhone Poulenc Contract*

Suttons Transport

Suttons Transport Group Limited	Head Office Gorsey Lane Widnes Cheshire WA0 0GG United Kingdom

Tel: 00 (44) 151 420 2020
www.suttons-group.com

Suttons Tankers	Gate House Bon Lea Industrial Estate Wilson Street Thornaby TS17 7AR

Tel: 00 (44) 1642 606160

Suttons Tankers	1203 Hedon Road Hull HU9 5LY

Tel: 00 (44) 1482 705366

Suttons Tankers	c/o ERF (Strathclyde) Ltd 30 Clydesmill Drive Clydesmill Industrial Estate Cambuslang Glasgow G32 8RG

Tel: 00 (44) 141 642 0011

Suttons Tankers	Cranberry Depot Gretna DG16 5HQ	Tel: 00 (44) 845 0200370
Suttons Distribution	Elton Head Road St Helens WA9 5BW	Tel: 00 (44) 1744 81611
Suttons International	North Trading Building Noorderlaan 133 B2030 Antwerp Belgium	Tel: 00 (32) 54000333
Suttons International	Kunsterwerkerstrasse 183 45136 Essen Germany	Tel: 00 (49) 163 2657463
Suttons International "Le Vaisseau"	120 Blvd Amiral Mouchez 76600 Le Harve France	Tel: 00 (33) 235 24 76 11
Suttons International	Unit D, 9/F Long Life Mansion 1566 Yan An West Road Shanghai 2000052 China	Tel: 00 (86) 21 5258 6000
Suttons International	15 South Main Street Suite No 2 Edison New Jersey 08837 USA	Tel: 00 (1) 732 549 3535

Suttons International

15811 Heatherdale Drive
Houston
Texas 77059
USA   Tel: 00 (1) 281 280 9521

Suttons International

5th Floor
Kyodo Building (Kayabacho)
6-12 Nihonbashi - Kayabacho
1-Chome
Chou-Ku
Tokoyo 103 – 0025
Japan   Tel: 00 (81) 3 3663 7170

Suttons International

B30, 2nd Floor
Lorong Tun Ismail 1
25000 Kuantan
Pahang
Malaysia   Tel: 00 (60) 9 517 1006